EBURY PRESS

IF I'M HONEST

Sidhartha Mallya is an American-born, British-raised actor of Indian descent. He was born in Los Angeles, California, to Indian parents, who moved to England shortly before his first birthday. He attended Wellington College and then Queen Mary University of London, where he graduated with a BSc in business management. After a short career in the business world, Sidhartha made the switch to acting. He trained at the Royal Central School of Speech and Drama, University of London, graduating with an MA in acting. He made his feature film debut in the Netflix original *Brahman Naman*, which premiered at the 2016 Sundance Film Festival.

Aside from acting, Sidhartha's main focus has been on the promotion of mental health among the youth. In 2020, he launched an online series called 'ConSIDer This', which talks about the mental issues he has struggled with over the years and offers advice to the public on how to deal with such challenges. *If I'm Honest* is his first venture into the writing world.

IF I'M HONEST

A memoir of my mental health journey

SIDHARTHA MALLYA

EBURY
PRESS

An imprint of Penguin Random House

EBURY PRESS

USA | Canada | UK | Ireland | Australia
New Zealand | India | South Africa | China

Ebury Press is part of the Penguin Random House group of companies
whose addresses can be found at global.penguinrandomhouse.com

Published by Penguin Random House India Pvt. Ltd
4th Floor, Capital Tower 1, MG Road,
Gurugram 122 002, Haryana, India

First published by Westland Publications Private Limited in 2021
Published in Ebury Press by Penguin Random House India 2023

ISBN 9780143459927

Typeset by SÜRYA, New Delhi

www.penguin.co.in

This book is dedicated to anyone who has gone through anything, ever. You are not alone.

Contents

To Begin With...   1

1. Sid the Kid   14

2. Depressed to Blessed   48

3. The Force of Divorce   62

4. Lose the Booze   91

5. OCD and Me   114

6. Built on Guilt   136

7. Sad about Dad   153

8. (What Helped Me) Be Free   169

So to Conclude...   192

Acknowledgements   195

To Begin With...

If I'm honest, when I started brainstorming ideas for this book, the thing I found most difficult was the introduction. How should I start it? What should I include? Should I say this? Should I say that? What if it turns into one long rambling paragraph that doesn't really introduce anything? Well, guess what. It is just that. But on the positive side, at least now we've got that awkward first moment out of the way, so let me say hello and thank you very much for being here!

If we are meeting for the first time, then hi! My name is Sidhartha and I'm an actor who currently lives in Los Angeles. Like many people, I've dealt with a number of different events throughout my life that have impacted my mental health. These have ranged all the way from depression and OCD (obsessive-compulsive disorder) to feelings of guilt and loneliness. In 2016 I went through depression and that's when my self-work started. Since then it's been a journey of self-discovery and self-reflection that has involved not only looking at the issues themselves, but also where they might have stemmed from and how they have affected me in different ways through the course of my life.

This book is me sharing my experiences and story with you in an open, honest and transparent manner. I am super passionate about mental health awareness, having seen the impact that looking after my own mental well-being has had on my day-to-day life. Everything I talk about in this book, whether it's the issues themselves or the events from my past that led to the issues, are things that only came to light after I started my mental health journey in 2016. I hope the book not only serves to amuse where it can, but also educates about various issues and how they can manifest; I hope it can inspire others to go on their own journey. Thank you for joining me.

A year ago, writing a book like this wouldn't have even crossed my mind. But it's funny how life tends to play out when you keep yourself open to all the possibilities.

Back in August 2018, I decided to stop drinking. (There's going to be an entire chapter on this and why I stopped, so I won't get into it now.) On the one-year anniversary of the day I stopped, I decided to post a brief Instagram story highlighting a few of the reasons I gave up alcohol. The response I received was mind-blowing. Thousands of people reached out to me, saying how much my message resonated with them and that they themselves felt the way I did. What struck me the most, however, was how many of them said that by hearing my admission, they themselves felt inspired to make changes when it came to alcohol, something they previously might not have felt they could do.

Just to give you a heads-up, my family has been one of the biggest producers of alcohol in the world for a number of years. It is a family business that had started with my grandfather and, before I went into entertainment, it was an industry I was being groomed to enter as well. Now here I was, this chap from an alcohol-producing family talking openly about how he'd stopped drinking! While this might have confused a few people (and my grandpop was probably tossing in his grave), it seemed to give many others the encouragement that if I could hit the bottle on the head, so could they. This really got me thinking: If I was able to reach and potentially help so many people by simply being open and honest about my own experiences with alcohol, maybe I could continue to help by being open and honest about some of the other issues I've gone through in my life as well.

So at the beginning of 2020, I decided to do a series of Instagram videos called ConSIDer This (catchy name, right? I came up with it all by myself), and in each ten-minute episode I spoke about a different mental health issue I'd gone through and how it had affected me in the course of my life. The idea wasn't to be preachy, but just to share in an open and transparent manner some of my personal experiences in the hope that maybe I could help and inspire others going through similar things. The reception the series received was insane. I had been taken aback by the response to my post on my one-year anniversary of no alcohol, but this reached a whole new level beyond even my wildest imaginings. (As you will find out, I have a pretty wild imagination.) People were reaching out from all parts of the globe to say how they could relate and how nice it was to hear someone talk about things from a personal point of view.

After seeing the impact I had made by simply shooting a bunch of videos on my iPhone, I vowed to continue doing whatever I could to shine a light on mental health and struggle. That led me to do a bunch of interviews, podcast appearances, magazine pieces and finally this book, which is really just an extension of the ConSIDer This series. Before you put the book down and log on to Instagram instead, don't worry. There is a whole bunch of content that I haven't included in the videos. I haven't made you pay for something you could watch online for free!

So what do I hope to achieve with this book? Apart from what I've already mentioned, I hope to get across a few key messages.

It's okay to be open and talk about our issues surrounding mental health

I decided to continue focusing on my own battles in this book for two reasons. First, because the ConSIDer This series helped me see that people seem to really appreciate hearing about personal experiences. Second, to show that it's OKAY to be open, honest and vulnerable, and to openly embrace and speak about our pain. In the world we live in today, many people feel as though they *have* to portray an image all the time of being 'super happy' and 'super positive', even if it doesn't match what they are really going through on the inside. A lot of this is down to the influence social media plays in our day-to-day lives and the number of posts that pop up in our feeds, spreading what has come to be known as 'toxic positivity'. (If you don't know what this is, Google it. It's a real thing!) While I think it's great to send forth positive vibes and have a positive mindset, much of this positivity doesn't actually stem from a place of truth, but serves to mask what's really going on for the person on the inside. This can be dangerous beyond anything most of us think.

I could easily write this book to tell you how great my life has been (because for the most part it has been a pretty good ride) and how strong and positive I am. And that I don't ever feel sad, or have never had any doubts or insecurities or worries or fears. But if I did this, I would be straight up bullshitting both you and myself. The truth is that, like all of us, I do have doubts, insecurities, worries and fears. I do at times feel sad and low. And most important, I do experience pain. Being human means dealing with and experiencing a whole range of emotions and feelings, including ones that society might deem 'negative' or 'bad'. Therefore, I think it's important to share these experiences with the world, to show that it's totally acceptable to be open and embrace every part of life.

There are already enough people who will go out of their way to tell you how everything in their lives is all unicorns and roses. There are way less people, however, who are actually willing to take the mask off and talk about what's going on underneath. What they struggle with. What their fears are. Why they feel the way they do. And it is this side of my life that I feel not only a duty to share, but also a willingness because it's my truth and authentic self.

Who knows, maybe when I'm old enough to retire I'll do a memoir that is a reflection of the 'good old days' and some of the 'wilder' times. But at this point in time, given where we are as a society and what's going on in the world, the experiences I've chosen to share in this book will hopefully serve to be more meaningful and potentially helpful.

Mental health comes in a number of different forms, not just depression, and no issue is too big or too small

If you ask someone what comes to mind when you say mental health, they will probably say, 'Mental health means you are depressed.' Most likely, I would have been one of those people had I been asked this before I started my self-work. While depression is clearly one of the more widely recognised mental health issues, it is not the only one by far. As I've come to learn, mental health has a number of different forms and mental ailments can present themselves in a number of different ways. Things such as OCD, loneliness, feelings of guilt or even being a child of divorce can all have an effect on mental well-being. So many of the things I've felt I would once never have categorised as mental health-related issues, even though now, looking back, it seems so obvious. To give you a quick example, I have suffered with OCD my whole life. As you will come to see, it caused me major amounts of psychological and emotional distress. But until I started to research and work on my OCD, I would never have thought it was a mental health-related condition. I probably would have just put my compulsive behaviour down to being a bad habit! This goes to show that much of the time we can potentially miss an issue because it doesn't fit within our preconceived notions of what mental health is or looks like.

The second part of this is that no issue is 'too big' to deal with and no issue is 'too small' to deserve attention. There are many areas in life where people will say 'size matters', but mental health isn't one of them! A lot of the time, there will be no acknowledgement that there is a mental health issue because it simply doesn't appear to meet the levels of severity someone believes it needs to in order to be classified as a problem. Many people I've come across feel that unless you are on the verge of a breakdown or feeling suicidal, an issue might not be worth dealing with. This is something I've definitely thought before. But as I learnt, things can affect us even if they don't 'seem' that severe on the surface.

No one is immune from suffering issues of mental health

Mental health doesn't discriminate. No one is immune to it. It can affect everyone at all stages of life, regardless of wealth, gender, ethnicity, upbringing or success.

There can sometimes be a belief that only 'certain people' have mental health issues and if you come from a life of perceived privilege, there is no way you could suffer. Even more dangerous than this is the belief that there is no way you have the *right* to suffer. This is certainly a belief I've had aimed at me at certain times from those who could never understand how someone 'like me' (whatever the hell that means) could suffer from anything, let alone a mental health-related condition. And I know I'm not alone here. How many of you reading this right now have had this said to you, 'What do you have to be depressed about? Your life is great!'

The truth is no matter how 'great' your life might appear to be (and by what yardstick do we measure 'great' anyway?), no one is immune from mental health-related issues regardless of age, gender, upbringing, financial status, the school they went to, the clothes they wear—anything. Things might look different on the outside, but on the inside we are all the same.

It's okay to seek help

Growing up I was a super stubborn human being. (For the sake of argument, let's just say it's because I'm a Taurus, okay?) The idea of asking for help for anything would have been a joke to me. Like many young people, I thought I knew everything and could do everything myself and I shared in the belief that vulnerability is weakness. Well, here I am today, at my good old age of thirty-four and I hold my hands up and say, 'I didn't know everything, and I still don't.' I don't have all the answers and I certainly don't always have the strength to deal with things alone. And since accepting that it's okay to not know things, to be vulnerable, to feel scared, to seek help, I've been able to let my guard down and get the help I need. Seeking help when I went through depression not only helped me deal with what I was experiencing, but also opened up a whole world of discovery that has since helped me deal with all the other issues I've faced through my life.

Many people find it hard to seek help even though in the back of their minds they know it's the right thing to do. This is partly because of the stigma that sadly still remains around mental health. This stigma often makes it seem unacceptable for someone to suffer a mental health-related issue, and worse, to seek help. For some reason, if someone admits to having a problem or gets help, they can quickly be labelled 'crazy' or 'unstable'.

Why should that be the case? We don't start labelling others if they break a bone or come down with the flu, so why should those who suffer mental ailments be classified differently? If you had a toothache, you would go a dentist. If you had a fever, you would go to the doctor. So why shouldn't you go to the appropriate specialist for help if you are suffering from something mental? By sharing my experiences of seeking help, I hope I can show that not only is it okay to get help, but it is also very much encouraged. Because what I've learnt is that allowing yourself to lower your guard and be vulnerable is actually the greatest show of strength there is. Had I not done that, I certainly wouldn't be in the position I am in today to not only deal with my issues, but talk about them as well.

There also certainly wouldn't be a book about it!

You are not alone

If by reading what I've written above, you, like me, now have a Michael Jackson song running through your mind, I do apologise. But seriously, if there is one thing that a person who might be suffering a mental health-related issue can take away from this book, it is that *you are not alone*. I know it can seem that way at times, as if you are the only person in the world who is struggling and no one else could possibly be going through something similar or understand it either. But there are often a lot more people than we think who can relate to us and the pain we experience. By sharing my journey, I hope I can help others feel less alone and more understood and seen.

Often, people aren't looking for answers or solutions to their problems, just someone they feel they can identify with and who can identify with them. One of the big things I found through the ConSIDer This series is that a lot of people appreciate hearing someone else talk about things they can relate to because it helps them feel less alone. One chap responded to my episode on OCD and said how great it was to hear someone else talk about something that he himself had suffered with, because growing up, he had thought he was the only one who suffered from such issues.

As they say 'strength in numbers', and when it comes to mental health, this is more important than ever.

⨍

So that is what I hope to do with this book and I thought the best thing would be to write it as a sort of memoir of my experiences and journey so far. I will share with you some of the main things I've struggled with throughout my life, what caused them and how much of it only became apparent to me after I started my self-work journey in 2016. I'll share anecdotes, I'll share stories and I'll give you as transparent a look into my life as I can. I'll also share some of the things I've found to be helpful as well as the positives I have taken away from each experience. The chapters are in no particular order and there is no particular structure to each one.

I do want to mention at this point (I probably should have led with this. Oh well!) that I am not a mental health professional and this is NOT a self-help book. I am just a normal human being sharing his story in the hope that it may inspire and help others going through similar things. Therefore, I ask that you please read it with an open mind. You may not resonate or agree with everything I'm saying, but please remember that the person behind the words is a real human being who hurts, feels and bleeds just like you.

This book is also not a complaint or a cry for sympathy or anything like that. It is just an open and honest reflection of the experiences and parts of my life that shaped me into who I am today.

I live my life by a simple motto: 'If you can make one person smile every day, you have made the world a better place.' Too often people believe that they must accomplish something grand in order to make the world a better place. This is why they don't believe they have the ability to make a difference. But really, the little everyday things each of us can do have the power to make the world better. So if this book can help just one person smile and feel less alone, then I've done my part to help make this world a better place and the book is a success.

one

Sid the Kid

So you're still with me. Great! I thought the best thing to do first is to tell you about who I actually am and where I come from, seeing that we are going to spend the next hundred pages or so together. The idea is to give you a look into my background and past, and the way my upbringing and certain events from my life had an impact on me. As this could be a book in itself, I'm only going to focus on the events that either had a profound effect on me at the time or the things I would later discover to be the root cause of some of my mental pain.

Early life

I was born in Los Angles to Indian parents, but moved to the UK when I was less than a year old.

My mom was an Air India flight attendant who came from a middle-class Bohri Muslim family. She was the youngest of three daughters and had more cousins than there are days in a month. She grew up in a big joint family, which meant that during her childhood she was always surrounded by people.

My dad was a very well-known Indian businessman. He was the only child of his parents and took over the business from his father at the age of twenty-seven when my grandfather unexpectedly passed away. Even though my dad was so young at the time, I've often been told me how great he was at what he did.

I realise I've been talking about them in the past tense, so let me just say, to avoid confusion, that at the time of writing this, they are both still alive!

They met each other on a flight, which I find very sweet. Call me old-fashioned, but given the digital age we live in today, I like the idea of actually meeting a person in person! But I digress.

So yes, my parents met and I am the only child through their marriage. As a child I had what would widely be considered a fortunate upbringing—from a material point of view at least. We lived in a huge house out in the English countryside. We had a tonne of domestic help and finances were never an issue. It was a very comfortable existence. Now I'm sure some of you are probably wondering at this point, well, if this guy had such a 'fortunate upbringing' what struggles could he have had? But as I said in my introduction, this is actually why I wanted to include this information: to highlight the fact that just because someone comes from a certain background, it doesn't mean they can't have suffered mentally. I think we're very quick to make judgements based on economic background and circumstances and we sometimes forget that everyone is human and can go through the same things.

If I seem a little defensive about this point, it's because being judged for my upbringing is something I've dealt with my whole life. This caused me feelings of guilt and turned into a complex I'm still dealing with today. As you'll come to see, guilt has been one of the major things I've struggled with over the years, and trying not to feel guilty about the life I was born into has been a real challenge for me. I'll be honest and say I was even a little apprehensive about including my background in this book for fear that I would somehow lose credibility in your eyes and be judged for the perceived privilege I come from. But a couple of weeks before writing this, I spoke with a spiritual healer who told me I needed to forgive myself for my background in order to move on peacefully. So let's just say that writing this and telling you where I come from is actually a step forward on that journey.

When I was a kid, my dad was my idol and all I wanted to be was like him when I grew up. I always remember him having a larger-than-life personality. He certainly enjoyed the good life and he played as hard as he worked. But given the amount he worked, why shouldn't he have? If you're going to put in hours working well, you might as well enjoy it. And that my dad did. He lived life to the fullest.

(Side note: One thing I would come to learn later in life is that success unavoidably comes with a price. When you become a recognisable face with as forceful a personality as my dad's, there will inevitably be people who will despise you as much as there will be people who love you. What happens then is that you become a target. But I'm getting ahead of myself. Let's get back to where we were!)

It was always instilled in me that one day I would join the business and take over from him. At the time, I loved that idea. I have memories of going into his office and sitting behind his desk, pretending to be some big-shot CEO, although I had no clue what that even was! Sadly, though, my dad wasn't there all that often because of his work commitments, so the time I actually got to spend with him in person was limited. I would soon find out that there were other reasons he wasn't there as well, but we'll come to that.

In terms of personality, I was a playful and overly energetic child. (This remains true even today.) And if I'm being totally honest, I was a handful. I remember once being likened to Dennis the Menace, which

I would say was a pretty fair comparison. I liked to have fun and I was always up to something or another. To give you an example, on one occasion, I locked one of my dad's secretaries in the office and ran away with the key. I thought this was highly amusing and being very proud of what I had pulled off, I went and gave the key to my dad. Now you're probably thinking what came next was a dressing down and a good smacking, but it was quite the opposite. The old man seemed to find my little stunt just as amusing as I did and he kept the key with him and that poor woman locked in the room for about half an hour. (*Disclaimer* No one was hurt during this episode.) This really summed up the relationship I had with him at that age. It was close and playful. Something that hasn't always been the case as the years have gone on.

My parents were generous and I was fortunate to be given many things growing up. The newest toys, clothes, nice holidays which, when you're a six-year-old, mean the world to you. All this kept me busy and amused. I'm sure a few of you are thinking, 'What a spoiled brat!', and if I'm honest, you're probably right. When my dad came home after being away for a while, he always brought a tonne of gifts. He would then rope in everyone from his office to play bingo with me and he would ensure I always won. The reason I mention this point is that when you're that young, you really don't value human connections as much as you value material possessions. And I think the sort of gifts I was given would either paper over the cracks or superficially fill the void I felt by not having my dad there on a constant basis.

My parents got divorced when I was around nine and although I didn't really feel the effects of it at the time, this was the catalyst for many of the issues I've dealt with throughout my life. Feelings of loneliness and abandonment stemmed off the back of the divorce, amongst other things. As I've grown older, I've realised that growing up with an absent parent had major psychological effects on me and I carried that trauma for years. Those of you who come from divorce or have gone through a divorce yourselves will know what I'm talking about. I think divorce is one of those interesting points when it comes to mental health because to many people, divorce isn't seen as that big a deal. But as you will know if you've experienced it, it can wound you deeply and leave scars.

Looking back, I think it's clear that as playful as I was, I developed a lot of anger due to the divorce and my poor mother had to bear the brunt of it. Being an only child meant two things. One, that I had to create my own fun. And two, that I had to deal with the divorce on my own. These two things led to me to develop an overly active imagination which was the closest thing I had to a sibling or,

I guess, the closest thing I had to comfort. This doesn't mean I had an imaginary friend. (I actually had several.) But it did mean that I spent a lot of time in my own imaginary world to keep myself amused and, quite honestly, to feel safe. If you are the only child of your parents, you will know what I'm talking about. Not long ago, someone asked me when I got into acting. I initially said 2012, but then remembered all the imaginary characters I had created while growing up and realised that I had actually been acting my whole life! I came up with characters all the time and was invested in the world I created. If that wasn't acting, I don't know what is! For example, my favourite character was Raphael from the Ninja Turtles and any chance I would get to play him, I would. I remember being given a Raphael costume and taking a couple of forks from the kitchen (because they resembled his three-pronged weapon called a Sai) and running around the house stabbing things, particularly the ornamental pillows, pretending they were bad guys. Let's just say I didn't win any gold stars for my behaviour. Although I do think I should have got one for not losing an eye in the process.

At the time this all seemed to be just fun and games, but now I would also say that the imaginary worlds I created were also a form of escapism due to the divorce and a way for me to feel as though I was in control. It was also a way for me to cope with the loneliness I felt at times from being on my own.

There's going to be an entire chapter dedicated to the divorce later, so I don't want to give too much away right now. But very quickly, my parents got divorced and my dad remarried and had two daughters with his new wife, who are my half-sisters. The lady he married also had two children from a previous marriage, who effectively became my dad's kids as well. This new family of his was based in San Francisco, meaning that I started seeing my dad even less than I already did because I was living in the UK. As I would come to know, my dad had actually had this other family without me knowing about it for a number of years before I met them. So by the time I was introduced to them, the elder of the two half-sisters was already three years old. And there I had been thinking I was my dad's only child! This is something that I would later come to see affected me much deeper than I initially was aware of. At the time I actually thought it was amazing that I had this new family—I had gone from being an only child to having siblings. I got caught up in the novelty of it all and, for the first time in my life, I felt the comfort of being part of a big family. Obviously before this I was on my own, so I didn't know any different. Now suddenly I was exposed to this whole new world of siblings and, most importantly, connection.

The problem, though, was that as I continued to live with my mom, I could only see them in the school holidays. This constant coming and going between seeing them and then having to come back to my mother caused feelings of instability that I've dealt with throughout my life. Other issues also stemmed off the back of the divorce, in particular, in meeting this new family, which I will come to later.

Additionally, when we get into the chapter on divorce, I'm going to explore the psychological effects it had on both me and my mom in more detail because I don't think the implications of divorce on mental well-being—both in the child and the parents—are really appreciated.

Teenage years

Most of my teenage years were spent at boarding school. Despite not being the most popular kid in the class, I loved my time there. The school I went to, Wellington College, was an old-school British public school which had old-style buildings and acres of land. I felt like I was Harry Potter at Hogwarts!

Boarding school was great fun and I got up to quite a few antics, especially as I got older. Those who didn't go to boarding school don't seem to understand why someone would choose to send their child away; some have even likened it to being sent to prison. I can understand this point of view, but I feel that the independence you learn at boarding school can serve you for the rest of your life. It certainly has with me. But I know from a kid's point of view it really is one of those things you either love or hate. Kind of like Marmite. (That's a joke that only the British readers among you are going to get.) For me, boarding school was the best time of my life. I started boarding in middle school at the age of ten and continued to board at secondary school or high school. Because so many kids went from my middle school to the same secondary school, I ended up living with some of these guys for eight years. We messed around, sneaked girls into the dormitory, hid in the bushes to drink cheap cider, basically did all the tomfoolery that one would expect from a teenager in the early 2000s. It was fun.

But what I really loved about it was that I felt I was part of a family. When you don't have siblings, or at least ones who live with you full-time, your friends at boarding school are more like brothers. And being there gave me the sense of stability and belonging that I had been missing growing up on my own. As you will see, that feeling of being part of a family is something I've craved throughout my life. It is one of the reasons why I got into acting and entertainment because, for me, being on set is one of the closest feelings to being back at school.

In the classroom, I was, to put it mildly, useless. I was a very average student and I'm not sure I ever got an A grade in anything. I also had dyslexia. To be honest, I was way more interested in having fun than in studying. And this reflected in my report cards. I was literally just a child who wanted to have fun and play. If anybody ever wanted to find me, all they had to do was look out on one of the sports fields and there I would be, kicking a ball around, usually on my own. When I left my middle school, Papplewick, one of my teachers, told my mom that if there had been an award for 'cheerfulness', I would have won it. I think that comment summed up what I was like as a child: just someone who wanted to be happy and who wanted to play.

I also started an underground business at boarding school, selling Kingfisher Beer promotional wear. My family business was in the production of alcohol and Kingfisher was one of our brands. After each holiday I'd come back with a suitcase full of beer mugs, coasters and pens, you name it, and sell them to the younger kids. I made a pretty penny, but my reason for doing this wasn't to make money, but simply to have fun.

Personality wise, I was very argumentative. If a teacher or one of the prefects said something I didn't agree with, I made my opinion known and wouldn't back down. I know this makes me sound like a troublemaker and, to be honest, I was. One of the things I've come to learn since starting my self-work is that there is a big difference between being argumentative because of your ego and being a person with strong convictions that stem from a place of confidence. Back then, like most teenagers, it was ego that caused me to be so argumentative.

I wouldn't have been considered one of the most popular kids either. To use an American high school movie analogy, I wasn't a jock. But I also wasn't a geek. I sort of fell in the middle. I had a hard time talking to girls, despite being relatively good-looking (or so I was told). It was as if I forgot how to speak English when I was in their presence. I became like a puppy who would look around waiting for someone to tell me what to do!

If we want to talk about a few of the downsides to the boarding school experience, then I think it would be these.

First, one of the issues I have suffered with through my life has been OCD. While it didn't start at boarding school, it grew into a pretty big monster while I was there. Apart from the obvious mental distress and time-wasting that the compulsions caused me, I was also often ridiculed by the other kids for what they viewed as weird behaviour (more details in the chapter on OCD). After all, I was living in that place 24/7, so everybody could see what I was up to. I wish I had known it was OCD at the time, because a) I think it could have been managed and I could have avoided the discomfort I lived with all the subsequent years, and b) It might have helped the other kids have more understanding and compassion for what I was dealing with.

Anyone who has OCD knows what a painful disorder it can be, especially if your compulsions are displayed in front of a bunch of other kids who don't understand what's going on. This can take a massive toll on you, and I hope more schools today give the disorder the attention it deserves in order to save kids the same pain I endured.

Second, while at boarding school, I subconsciously started to bury my emotions. I think when you live with a bunch of boys, you never want to show weakness or vulnerability. So you inadvertently put up a guard. The problem, though, is that the feelings you bury don't just disappear and they will eventually emerge in some way, shape or form. It took me until I started serious acting training years later to reconnect with my emotions and learn to let my guard down. Who knows, if I hadn't gone down this career path, I may well have stayed a guarded individual and not open enough to write a book like this!

The final 'negative' (I use inverted commas here because I don't actually think any of this was necessarily negative, just an experience) is that boarding school wired me to have a hard time switching off. While I was there, I was pretty much on a schedule from 7 a.m. to 10 p.m. each day. We even had a half day of classes on Saturday, meaning that there was always something to do. At the time this was a benefit, as I was never bored. But this constant *doing* wired my brain to believe I always have to be on the go. This was something I struggled with until very recently. If I ever took some time off or hit the pause button even for a second, my mind would tell me I was being lazy and guilt would kick in. The reason I mention this is because it had an effect on my relationships with both friends and girlfriends.

University

In 2005 I started at Queen Mary, University of London, for my undergraduate degree. University was the first time I ever felt like my own person. Of course with hindsight, who I thought I was then is very different to who I am today. Nonetheless, I felt a freedom when I went to university that I had never felt before. I think that's because I was the only person from my school to go to my university, which meant I could really reinvent myself and be whoever I wanted to be (which ended in being a degenerate for the next three years!). Suddenly I was confident. I joined the hockey team. I became popular. I went from being 'average Joe' to 'Jack the lad' in a very short period of time. Sometimes just a change in environment and a fresh start can make all the difference.

Having already have been away from home for seven-odd years at boarding school, going to university and living on my own wasn't that big a deal for me. In fact I loved it. On my first day, as

I went into my halls of residence, I saw a bunch of other eighteen-year-olds sitting in their rooms and crying. I wondered, 'Why are these kids crying? This should be such a liberating feeling.' And it then hit me that for a lot of them, this was the first time they had ever been away from their parents or out of their house. So I guess my experience from boarding school put me ahead of the curve when it came to independence.

I also remember one kid walking in with a six pack of beer and I was like, 'Whoa, whoa, whoa, what are you doing? You're going to get into trouble.' And he looked at me like I was an idiot. I had to remind myself that I was no longer in school, and was allowed to do this. So I went promptly to the off-licence and bought as much alcohol as I could to stock the little fridge in my room. From that point on, my room came to be known as 'Bar Sid', and over the next year it became the spot where people pre-gamed before the night's festivities. This is just an example of the freedom I felt.

As I mentioned earlier, it had sort of been drilled into me from a very young age that I would eventually join the family business, I guess because that's what good Indian boys do. So I went to university to study business management. (Quick sidenote here: Out of the six universities I had applied to, I'd been rejected by five. Queen Mary was the only one to make me an offer, so it wasn't like I had much of an option.) I actually applied to do politics, but didn't get the grades at A Level, so through a process called 'clearing', I ended up on the business management course instead. Now that I'm on a whole different career path, it doesn't seem to matter all that much, but at the time it was devastating.

I pretended my very best to study, but let's be honest, university was basically a three-year bender for me. Lots and lots of drinking, with minimal study. During my time there, I was captain of the men's field hockey team, although we were more of a drinking society that happened to play a little hockey, than a hockey club that had a few social drinks. Perhaps more fittingly, I was also the chairman of an underground drinking club that a group of us had founded called the 'Tens'. Again, all I wanted to do was play and have fun.

Sadly, they don't give credit for these extracurricular activities, or I would have left with a PhD. Anyway, after three years, ten thousand pints of beer, five thousand Sambuca shots and enough doner kebabs to feed a small nation (these numbers are not accurate), I graduated with a BSc (although a 'BS' would've been more applicable to me) in business management. I also met some of my closest friends at university, so that was the best thing to come out of my time there. It's strange because when I left my secondary school, Wellington, I was like, 'Yeah, I'm going to stay in touch with everyone forever!', but in reality, I'm probably in touch with three people. It's my university friends that I am a lot closer to. They say you meet your best friends at university, or at least the friends you will stay with for the rest of your life, and I've certainly found that to be true.

Work and move to India

After graduating from Queen Mary, I didn't go straight into the family business. Instead I worked for a company called Diageo in London. Diageo was another massive alcohol company and I was assigned to work on the beer brand Guinness. The overall plan was for me to eventually end up in India with the family, but my dad and I agreed that it would be best for me to have some work experience with an outside company before joining ours. So I started working as an assistant brand manager for Guinness in their marketing department, with a focus on the Guinness Premiership, the professional rugby league in the UK that Guinness was the title sponsor of at the time.

My year at that company was very enjoyable and I have some great memories. But it was a challenge to settle into corporate life, partly because I found it very difficult to sit behind a desk and focus for eight hours a day (back then I could barely sit still for eight minutes) and also because I found it very difficult to shake off the carefree, university attitude

I still had. These two things led me to become what was known as a 'weekend warrior'. I would spend my weekdays counting down to Friday night when I could hit the booze with my friends. We would go out on a Friday night and continue boozing all the way until late on Sunday. I would be so hungover on Monday that for the next two to three days, I would operate at a sub-optimal level, to put it mildly. And then, of course, by the time I felt somewhat myself again, the weekend was upon us and the booze train was ready to leave the station.

One thing I've come to see is that apart from not taking responsibility, I also did not value life back then. By constantly living in anticipation of the weekend, I was missing out on the present and on enjoying each and every day. Now, having done my self-work, it's clear that 'not valuing life' was the worst thing I could have done. Human beings have a finite time on this planet, so it's important to value every moment. When I look back, if that year taught me anything, it was to be more responsible, but more important, to live fully each and every day and to value every moment.

After my year at Diageo came to an end (believe it or not, I wasn't fired. It was only meant to be a year), I made the inevitable move to India. I could probably write an entire book just on my experiences of living in India. Even though I was only there for a couple of years, it honestly felt like a lifetime. And if I'm going to be completely transparent with you, it was probably the most challenging two years of my life. I really didn't enjoy the experience and I think a lot of it had to with the fact that I just wasn't prepared for the life that was about to be presented to me and the world I was about to enter.

Having Indian parents meant I had constantly visited India during my childhood. So the place itself wasn't alien to me. There is, though, a big difference between visiting a place a few times a year on vacation and actually living in that place full-time. So as familiar as I was with the country, I wasn't fully prepared to make it my home.

A big reason for this was down to how my move to India actually came about because it did not happen as it had been originally planned. After I left Guinness in September, the plan was for me to spend another year working in the UK, this time for one of our companies, before moving to Mumbai. As that job wasn't due to start till the new year, I had a little time off until January, which I spent a part of in India. Then over the new year's holiday, I had a chat with my dad and we decided that instead of going to work for this company in the UK, I should just move to India and start working there because that was the endgame anyway.

At the time, this made sense to me. I knew that spending an extra year in the UK was just putting off the inevitable move to India. So with that in mind, mixed with basically just being caught in the moment and also being partly drunk (no joke, I had had a few beverages at the time of this conversation), I decided to make the move.

Until I moved to India, my entire life had been in England. My friends were there, my mom was there, and everything I knew and was comfortable with was there. Because I was so caught up in the decision to move and because it all happened so fast, I didn't allow myself to mentally process that my entire life was about to change. I didn't give myself adequate time and space to come to terms with the fact that it would mean leaving my friends, my mom and basically my life as I knew it behind.

Anyone who's had to move countries, whether for work or family reasons, will know that this sort of decision takes thought and planning. For me, it was a shotgun decision. In hindsight, not rushing the move might have helped me in the longer term. At the very least, taking the time to process what I was about to get into would have had a positive advantage and helped me mentally prepare for it.

So now I found myself in India suddenly living a life that was very different from what I was used to in the UK. Despite my Indian parents, I was really as British as Yorkshire pudding and I felt like a fish out of water. There were many differences I felt after the move, but two things really stuck out. First, the lack of freedom I felt. This was mainly due to living in a big family house again for the first time since I went to boarding school. In Indian culture it's very common for children to live with their parents or in big joint families, but for me, having grown up in the West and gone to boarding school when I was so young, it was a big culture shock.

The second thing to shock my system was the amount of attention I started to get through the media and members of the general public. I had known my family was fairly well-known and while I'd expected some attention, I wasn't prepared for the amount I received. Just like that, I became somewhat of a 'celebrity' (although there was really nothing to celebrate). There were articles about me in the press, I was shooting magazine covers for GQ and *People* and I was doing interviews. As a result of this 'fame', my ego blew up—partly because a part of me felt super cool and really enjoyed the attention and partly because a part of me felt like a fraud for the attention I was getting, haven't not really achieved anything to deserve it. I had this constant inner conflict going on.

To mask these feelings, and this conflict, I decided to portray myself as this 'British guy who gives zero fucks about what people think about him' and who 'isn't afraid to speak his mind and ruffle a few feathers'. (Believe me, I ruffled more than just a few feathers during my time in India.) The problem with this, though, was that it wasn't truly me at all. It was just my ego putting up a guard to mask my deeper insecurities as well as the pain I felt from being in India in the first place. Of course, at the time I hadn't done the self-work and self-discovery I've done today, so I didn't have the tools to understand that this wasn't my authentic self. I just genuinely assumed that was who I was. I think that, often, we believe we are being authentic and coming from a place of truth, when actually our behaviour stems from a place of fear. And when this happens, it becomes problematic because one ends up constantly trying to defend oneself and this image that has been created. This was certainly the case with me. Because the persona I was portraying didn't come from a place of security and truth, it came across as arrogance and defiance. It made me short-tempered, it made me irritable and this came through in my relationships as well as in the interviews I gave. (Even to this day I can't read some of the interviews I had given because they are so cringeworthy.) All because I was constantly trying to defend myself. Because of that persona, some of you reading this book might have a different image of who I am. All I can say to that is that back then I was operating from a place of fear and ego and today I'm operating from a place of truth and my soul.

A great thing to have come out of my self-work is that I am now at a place where I don't feel I have any points to prove to anyone, where the only person I need to focus on is me. Since getting to this point, it has made life so much easier to live, because I'm no longer wasting energy trying to uphold an image that isn't my true self.

One of the most confusing things I had to learn to deal with was reading stuff about myself in the press, particularly stuff that simply wasn't true. For example, an article at the beginning of 2010 stated that I had—and this is no joke—flown to Tanzania to select a specific diamond for an engagement ring that I was planning to give someone. I got phone calls from family members, including my mother, asking whether this was true. Of course it wasn't and I remember at the time sort of being quite amused by a story like this, but also on a deeper level being confused as to how something like this could be written. I felt a sense of frustration that lies were able to be said so freely and that I really didn't have much power to change the narrative.

Little did I know that this was only scratching the surface of the things I would go on to read in subsequent years. This example pales in comparison to some of the vindictive, nasty and downright vicious stuff I read about myself during my time in India. Things which definitely took a mental toll on me, and which made my ego feel the need to defend itself even more.

I was definitely not at peace in India. And because I didn't really enjoy myself, I drank way too much and partied way too much as an escape. There is a whole chapter dedicated to my relationship with alcohol, and how it affected me and the way I used it, so I won't say too much here.

At that point in my life, I was lost. I didn't know myself and was in an environment where I didn't want to be. This was where I believe I first encountered depression. But I didn't know I was depressed at the time. Only since going through depression in 2016 and getting to know more about it did I come to learn that one can actually be depressed without knowing it. My behaviour in India definitely had all the signs of someone who was depressed without being aware of it.

But as miserable as I was, my time in India might be the most important two years of my life because it made me see the sort of person I didn't want to be. In life we have choices and we can choose who we want to be and who we don't want to be. And by seeing the person I was in India, totally run by his ego, I can today choose to not be that and instead be someone who is run by his soul and who embraces vulnerability and openness. So as much as I didn't enjoy the experience of being in India, it certainly was a very important part of my life.

Change in career

In India, I also started to feel something of an identity crisis. I was being seen as 'Vijay Mallya's son' and very rarely as my own person. I felt I wasn't taken seriously and I had a need to prove myself because I was constantly being judged. I remember once saying in an interview that 'the name Sidhartha is a hell of a lot more important to me than the name Mallya'. While I still believe this to be true, I was saying it from a very defensive place back then. Though it was not the only reason, this need to be recognised for being my own person contributed to me deciding to change career paths.

I should also mention that during my time in India, my relationship with my dad wasn't the best it's ever been. We both have very strong personalities and they clashed. The deep resentment and unprocessed feelings I had towards him that I'd been bottling up unconsciously for all the years since my parents' divorce started to come to the surface. It was a struggle on a personal level so, from a business point of view, it made me want to pursue something outside the family.

Why acting? Well, as I said earlier, I loved creating worlds and characters while I was a child as it gave me a way to use my wild imagination and deal with the loneliness I felt from being an only child of divorced parents. This passion for performing was reignited during my time in India. Whether it was the magazine photo shoots or the interviews or even hosting my own talk show for the Indian Premier League, I was definitely the happiest when I was in a situation where I was able to express myself creatively and freely. When I went to drama school in 2015, I remember my movement teacher, Anna, saying at my end of term assessment that when 'Sid is free, and having fun, he just shines and there's a playful glow to him. But when he is being told what to do, he sort of shuts off and closes off and doesn't really have much interest'. This was the most accurate assessment of myself I've ever gotten and so in line with my experiences of the corporate world. Put me behind a desk in an office and I close off. But put me in front of a camera, or on a stage with the freedom to express myself and I really shine.

I started getting great feedback for the creative stuff I was doing. I was told I had a presence that would work on screen. Hearing things like this fuelled my desire to pursue a path in entertainment. The simplest way of doing this would have been to try Bollywood. I was already in India, I knew people in the entertainment industry there and there were definitely opportunities for me as an actor. But I didn't want to explore this at the time because I didn't think I had the right sensibilities for Bollywood. Looking back, though, a big part of not exploring Bollywood was also that I was simply scared. I was scared that I would have been put under a microscope again and been viewed as just someone's son who got lucky because of who his dad was. I was scared that I wouldn't be taken seriously because of the family I came from and that the media who already enjoyed taking me apart would continue doing so. Funny, isn't it, how many decisions in life we actually make out of fear, even if we don't necessarily realise that fear is the driving force at the time? I was also a very stubborn person at that point in my life, so there was a part of me that was determined to make it somewhere else; away from where my family name meant anything. That led me to my decision to pursue my career in the United States.

As I'd been born in Los Angeles, I was already an American citizen, so moving there and working there wouldn't be a problem.

After mulling it over, I spoke to my dad about my desire to not only quit the family business but move to the other side of the world as well to pursue a completely different career path.

Just writing this makes me realise what a big decision it was. I remember saying to him that I didn't think I could build the business the way his dad and he had done because my heart wasn't in it. While on this point, let me say that I never had the opportunity to meet my dad's dad. But from what I hear, he was a great man with a brilliant business mind. He started United Breweries by buying up breweries that had been shut down due to prohibition. He was a genius in his own right and my dad inherited that business acumen from his old man. Between the two of them, they were able to establish and grow our business into an industry leader internationally. And I simply didn't feel I would be able to continue that legacy and gain the same success that they did. Not because I wasn't good enough, but because I just didn't have the same passion for it as they did. I believe passion is one of the most important qualities in life, and without it, it's very difficult to succeed in whatever you are trying to do, regardless of ability or talent.

A question I get asked a lot, especially by South Asians, is how did my dad take being told that I didn't want to be in the family business? I have to say he handled it extremely well. I know many parents, especially in the Indian community, would've dismissed such a notion and demanded that their kids continue to work in the family business and continue the legacy, even if it meant compromising their children's happiness. But at no point did my dad ever try to talk me out of it, or put any pressure on me to stay. What he said was the reason that he was able to spend eighteen hours a day in the office and work as hard as he did was that he loved what he did. And because he loved what he did, he was able to be successful at it. Therefore, I should find what I love to do. He also said he knew I would be a success because I was a very determined individual. I had recently completed the Mumbai marathon after only nine weeks of training and he used that as an example to prove that once I put my mind to something, he had no doubt that I would succeed.

I could not be more thankful to him for the support he gave me. To have me tell him point-blank that I had no interest in continuing what he and his father had built couldn't have been easy for him. But he was very, very supportive.

Others, however, were not as supportive. Certainly a few people made me feel guilty, made me feel as though I were a Judas or a Brutus and my actions were somehow treacherous.

I'm really happy that I got to experience the corporate world for a couple of years because it helped me figure out what I didn't enjoy. You don't know what you like or don't like until you experience it. Today I can say that I'm happy I made the change in career because I've experienced both sides.

I've always been an artist. Whether it's acting, making mental health videos or a writing a book, that's where my happiness lies. But I had to go through the corporate world to experience the life that I didn't want in order to see where my true passion lay.

In mid-2012, I moved to Los Angeles, all set to pursue a career in entertainment but not really knowing what it would entail. I signed with a big agency because they had a partnership with a company that was looking after some of my commercial interests in India, and with a manager as well. I enrolled in an acting studio and started taking acting classes and auditioning. Looking back, I will say that like a lot of people who arrive fresh-faced in LA, I don't think I valued or respected what it really takes to be an actor as much as I should have at the time. I thought things would happen for me a lot quicker than they did.

I remember having a chat with my manager about this. She said, 'Look, there is a long process and a hard way of doing this, which is auditioning, or there's an easy way to do this and that is just to fund your own content.' I was crushed by this. Because I'd been thinking that I was going to make it on my own; that I was going to succeed without the help of my family. And now I was being told, well, there's a shortcut to the top if you just get your family to fund your stuff. At the time this made me feel disheartened, as though I would never be able to be my own person or shake off the baggage that came with my surname. I'm so happy that I didn't cave and that I stuck with it and did things in what I call the 'right' way. Maybe I'm not as far along in my career as I would have been had I followed her advice, but at least I feel I've paid my dues and not cut corners.

After being in a few short films and web series (web series back then were basically YouTube videos, not the streaming services of today!), I shot my first feature film in 2014. It was called *Brahman Naman* and it was basically what they called a 'sex comedy'. (No, not pornography, although that was the first thing that came to mind when I saw the description!) It's about a bunch of college students growing up in 1980s Bangalore. The irony was that the film was actually shot in India, and not just that, it was set in Bangalore where my family is from. I remember going there for the shoot and just having the best time of my life. Being on set, being around other creative people, was a real high for me. Being able to express myself was such a liberating feeling and one that validated my choice to pursue this career. For the first time since I was young, I had that childlike playfulness back and I felt like my authentic self.

After the film, I decided to go to drama school in the UK for professional training, as I wanted to take my craft to the next level and be the best I could be. I felt good about the training I had had so far, but I wanted more. If I'm honest, though, there was still a part of me that felt I had to prove myself, even though I had just shot a feature film; that people would say, 'Oh, he only got a role because he is the son of so-and-so.' So I felt that a proper Master's degree from one of the world's best drama schools would close that conversation.

I applied and got into the Royal Central School of Speech and Drama on the Master's programme for acting. Just getting in that programme was a huge achievement for me because British drama schools are exceptionally tough to get into, given that there are so few places on offer for the number of applicants. I had to go through an assessment, a couple of auditions and an interview. The day I got the email saying I was being offered a place was one of the best days of my life. Partly because I was so excited to have been accepted and partly because my ego felt I had achieved something on my own.

The year at drama school was one of the most transformational years of my life. It opened me up emotionally. It got me in touch with myself and I really got to know me. Drama school was also where I started my journey with mental health, or at least consciously started my journey with mental health. As I said earlier, I had been depressed without knowing it when I was in India and even after moving to Los Angeles, I remained in that depression. A friend of mine said not long ago, 'Sid, it's so nice to see how much you've changed because when I saw you back in 2013/2014, I could just see pain behind your eyes, as if you had a dagger stuck in your side.'

It's interesting, isn't it, what others can see though you might not be aware of it yourself? But going to drama school got me in tune with my body and my emotions and got me to really see the issues I was going through.

While I was at drama school, my dad started to go through some—let's just say, legal—complications involving his business and the government of India. Over the last five years, he has been in a battle with the Indian government who has accused him of fraud, deception, money laundering and collusion, amongst other things, which he strongly denies. It's had him arrested in the UK and released on bail and attend court on numerous occasions. It's caused him huge amounts of stress on a daily basis. And it's caused me much anguish to witness. There is a whole chapter on the situation and the mental effects this whole ordeal has had on me because it's been draining to say the least!

Because my father is a public figure, these complications have been widely circulated and publicised in the media. It was very difficult for me to see these sorts of things written about him and receive messages from people who had read the same things. At drama school, I was able to use performance and the characters I portrayed as an outlet for the pain I felt. But when school came to an end in late 2016, I no longer had this outlet on an everyday basis. That's when the depression hit me. That's when I sought professional help.

It was at this point that my journey of self-work started. That journey has included working with therapists, stopping alcohol, working on my OCD and a whole range of other things that have helped me deal with pain that I unknowingly had going on inside me for years.

To conclude...

Everything in life can be viewed as a negative or a positive, depending on the lens through which you view it. Some of you who read this chapter might believe I've had a blessed life with nothing to complain about. Others may resonate with the pain I've felt over the years. Either way, what I've grown to appreciate is that everything in my life up until this point has been an experience and is my truth. It has all shaped me into the person I am today—the person writing this book. In the following chapters, I will go into more detail about the things and events that have impacted me the most in my life from a mental point of view.

What else should I include before we move to the next chapter? All right, my star sign is Taurus. My favourite colour is orange. My favourite food is sushi and my favourite person is my dog, Duke. He is looking at me as I write this to make sure I don't name anyone else. I love sports. I support Southampton football club. I hate elevators because I'm claustrophobic. And I'm petrified of sharks. I've broken three bones. Had over forty stitches. And enough x-rays to glow in the dark.

Hopefully now you feel you know me, so let's begin.

two

Depressed to Blessed

I feel blessed. I feel blessed to have been depressed. (Turns out I'm also a poet and I didn't know it.) But no, I say this because if I hadn't gone through the experience of depression, I don't know whether I would have started my self-work journey. So from that point of view, being depressed was a blessing.

If you had told the younger, stubborn me that I would be thirty-four years old and not only have been through depression, but would now also be openly talking about it, I would've asked you what you were smoking. Because I never would have believed that I could have been depressed, and I was so guarded that talking about my problems would have seemed so alien.

Before I get into my story, I think it's important to acknowledge how the world is talking a lot more about mental health today, particularly depression. It's great to see so many public figures doing their part to help end the stigma around the subject by sharing their own stories and experiences. Yes, there is still a long way to go, but it's great to see the path we're all on. What's most encouraging, though, is to see schools take mental health more seriously and educate kids about it from a younger age. When I was growing up, mental health was not something that any of my schools gave any attention to. If there had been more talk of it back then, I may have been able to detect many of my troubles earlier on. Not long ago I was talking to my cousin who has a young son at boarding school and he said that one of his son's classmates was going through depression. Not only was this child on medication, he openly talked about his experience with his classmates as well. While my first reaction was to feel for the lad, hearing this also filled me with hope. When I was in school, you had more chance of catching a brick in a spider's web than finding a child who was so open!

ƒ

So here is how my experience with depression unfolded. When I went to drama school in 2015, it opened me up and reconnected me with my emotions. The acting training I'd had in Los Angeles prior to this had also helped, but it was drama school that really took my openness to a level I had never felt before. While I was there, my dad's legal troubles started, which caused me internal pain. Had his troubles happened before I'd gone to drama school or even before I got into the world of acting, I'm sure I wouldn't have felt it as deeply as I did because I was disconnected from my feelings and my guard was up. But because that guard had been lowered and I was more connected, I felt the situation more than I might have in the past. This was a shock to my system in and of itself.

Towards the end of my time at drama school, I was cast in a short film to play an ex-heroin addict. My character was very dark and very troubled. I decided to go full-blown Christian Bale and lost about seven kilos for the role to get the physicality right. Playing a character like this also meant that I could use all the pain I was feeling from my dad's situation and use it in the expression of my character. It's been said that some of the greatest art comes from the depths of despair and this experience helped me see this is true. That's one of the great things about acting, or any form of art. It serves as a great channel for your emotions.

Then the shooting of that short film came to an end, meaning that the outlet I had was taken away, but the emotions and pain were still there. I spoke to the head of my course about this and she referred me to the school's on-site counsellor. Speaking to the counsellor about what I was going through was really my first experience of speaking to a mental health expert and it felt good to have found another outlet.

Drama school came to an end in the third quarter of 2016 and I suddenly found I had a lot of time to myself. The previous year had been so intense that I now felt something of a void.

At the same time, my dad's situation was getting worse, and I also started getting abusive messages because of it. Things such as, 'I hope your family dies' and 'I hope you go to jail'. Horrible things, which naturally had an emotional effect on me. Let me say at this point that anyone who says these sorts of messages don't affect them is either made of stone or is flat out lying. I think what happens when people leave negative comments on social media is that they forget there's a real person behind the photos who's actually reading what's been written. Too many people see comments on social media as throwaway lines and they don't quite realise the impact their comments can have.

So I would wake up in the mornings feeling lost and empty and like I had a lack of purpose in life. You know those Halloween films where you see zombies rise from the dead and they just wander around, not looking like they know what they are doing? That's basically what I was like. I was also experiencing a continuous low mood and sadness.

There were unexplained aches and pains, particularly in my shoulders, back and neck, and a continuous lack of energy, even though I was fit and athletic.

Every day I woke up feeling drained. I started avoiding my friends because meeting people would make me very irritable. I think the main thing that I felt during this time though was loneliness. Though I was in London and had all my friends and family there, I just felt alone and I couldn't understand why. Little did I know that all these things were signs of depression.

Often there is a misconception that the word depression only applies to a state where you can't get out of bed in the morning or you feel suicidal. But I learnt that simply isn't true. You can be depressed and not even realise it because you are still able to function. That is what was happening to me.

I kept trying to talk myself out of feeling this way. 'Come on, Sidhartha, snap out of it. You're young. You're healthy. You have great friends. You have a great family. You've just come out of one of the world's best drama schools. You have the world at your feet. You have all these opportunities. You're so fortunate. There are people in the world way worse off than you are. Stop feeling like this!' I would continuously run this monologue through my head and I would beat myself up in the hope that I would somehow magically snap out of it. But not only did it make me spiral even further down the rabbit hole, it made me feel super guilty as well for the way I was feeling

I quickly learnt that having great friends, a great family, roofs over our heads and food on our tables does make us fortunate. But not immune to mental health issues. If you take anything away from this chapter, let it be that you mustn't beat yourself up for what you are going through—you have the right to feel what you feel.

All of this came to a head at a friend's wedding in Europe. It was one of those big Indian destination weddings at a beautiful location. All my friends were there, and it was just three days of partying. There was great music, great food, lots of alcohol and I was with the people I loved. Basically it had all the ingredients for a twenty-nine-year old to have a great time! But all I felt in those three days was crushed inside. I remember this one point when we were on a bus to the dance rehearsal for the sangeet (I had somehow been roped into dancing, even though me dancing to Bollywood music is literally like watching Bambi on ice without the cuteness), I was sitting there feeling like my insides were being actually crushed by a massive vice. Everyone else on that bus was laughing and happy. While I did my best to join in, inside me there was a very different story happening to what was being portrayed on the outside.

I also remember at one of the events that night,

wandering around pretty much by myself, going from corner to corner, side to side of the massive nightclub we were in, feeling lost and alone amongst the sea of people having a good time. I'm sure friends of mine who were there that night will read this and be a bit surprised to hear how I was feeling, because I was masking what was going on inside. Again, I was going through my monologue: 'Stop feeling like this! Be happy. Smile. This is an amazing event. You've got your friends here. It's an amazing party.' But the more I tried to push happiness out, the more my body rejected it and the more low I felt.

When I came back to London after the wedding, everything that had been building up finally came out. It was a stereotypical British day: wet and cold and the sky was as grey as an elephant's arse. I lived in a duplex that had a staircase and I just sat there and broke down. I cried and cried and cried. The floodgates had literally opened—years of emotion came out!

Opposite the staircase was a mirror. When I looked up and saw my reflection, I shouted the same negative monologue that I had by now become something of an expert at delivering: 'Why are you feeling this way? You shouldn't be feeling like this! Stop it, stop it, stop it!'

Of course, my reflection wasn't giving me any answers, which wound me up even more. Really, the best way to describe how I was feeling was to use a reference from Harry Potter. (I'm a big HP fan.) In the Harry Potter books, characters called dementors guard the Azkaban prison, and these dementors suck the happiness out of everyone they come in contact with. As I sat there on the staircase crying, I felt like I had a dementor on my shoulder, sucking the life and happiness out of me. It was at that point that I realised I needed to do something about this; that it was no way to live. So I decided to seek professional help.

I saw my general practitioner and told him everything I was going through. He said I was depressed and referred me to a psychiatrist for a full evaluation. When I went to see the psychiatrist, I was clinically diagnosed with obsessive-compulsive disorder. I remember thinking, 'Yeah, no shit, Sherlock, I know I've got OCD, I could've told you that myself.' But honestly, what I thought OCD was and what I've come to learn it actually is, is very different. My understanding at that time barely scratched the surface. Since then I've learnt that obsessive-compulsive disorder has actually been at the heart of a lot of my pain and was central to the depression I was experiencing at the time. It has been something my therapist and I have worked on extensively over the past couple of years because it has been so prominent in my life.

My experience with the psychiatrist isn't something I remember fondly. I didn't ever feel comfortable talking to him. They say what makes a good doctor isn't necessarily the medical knowledge they have but their bedside manner. This chap didn't make me feel at ease. But in his notes of one of our sessions (there were three sessions in total), he said, 'Sid went on to reflect on his experience at boarding school where he felt he was conditioned to avoid looking at emotions and maintain control. By contrast, his recent acting training has had the opposite effect since participants are encouraged to explore their emotions and be in the present.'

I think that was the perfect summary of the change I had been going through since drama school and why I was feeling the way I did. As someone who liked to be very much in control, particularly of his emotions, I was now feeling things more deeply than I had ever done before, which made me feel out of control.

The psychiatrist prescribed antidepressants to help with my mood and the OCD, and I started taking Cipralex, a brand of SSRI antidepressant. If you are like me and are wondering what the hell SSRI is, 'SSRI' stands for 'selective serotonin reuptake inhibitor'. According to drugs.com, 'SSRI antidepressants are a type of antidepressant that work by increasing the levels of serotonin within the brain. Serotonin is a neurotransmitter that is often referred to as the "feel good hormone".' I took them for about three months and saw an improvement in my mood.

During this time, I went to a friend's wedding in LA. For the few days I was there, I stopped taking the antidepressants because I was drinking and didn't want to mix the two. I felt great at the wedding. I don't remember why, but I actually felt pretty happy. Given the fact that this was only a month or two on from the earlier wedding in Europe where I had felt crushed, this was a big change. So I thought to myself, perhaps there are more natural ways to regulate my mood than antidepressants. (Quick aside here: When I start taking the SSRIs, I forgot to tell my mom I was on them. She found out via an Instagram post I put up on World Mental Health Day two years later. It's safe to say this came as a bit of a surprise to her, so if any of you are taking medication, maybe tell your loved ones. All I can say is, I'm sorry, Ma!)

The other thing I was asked to do by the psychiatrist was see a therapist. Up until this point the counsellor at drama school was all I had experienced, so this was my first real experience with a mental health professional and I really didn't enjoy it. Her office was in one of those big London townhouse sort of buildings on Harley Street. I remember walking into her office and feeling uncomfortable from the get go. She sat opposite me with an iPad on which she made notes, which made me feel like I was being judged more than I was being helped. The environment really didn't make me want to open up.

When I'm asked about therapy, I say the most important thing is finding the right therapist. Someone who makes you feel comfortable, who makes you want to open up and talk. With therapy, you only get out of it as much as you're willing to put in, so if the person doesn't make you want to talk, your guard will be up and you won't get much out of it.

At the beginning of 2017, I moved back to Los Angeles and started to practice meditation through various apps. I was determined to find alternative coping mechanisms rather than continue with SSRIs. I was familiar with meditation because my end-of-year essay at drama school had been on the link between meditation and acting, but the thing I always found troubling was the constant worry of whether I was 'doing it properly'.

It was only when I found Transcendental Meditation (TM) that I became totally comfortable with it. TM didn't seem to have any rules and I think that took a great deal of pressure off me because I felt I couldn't do it wrong.

My mood had definitely improved by this point, but I felt I wanted to go deeper and explore the roots of my pain. So I decided to give therapy another go. My doctor referred me to a wonderful, caring person who was such a contrast to my experience back in London. I've worked with her for close to four years now and she has literally transformed me. Not only has she helped me open up and express myself more, she has guided me to look back at my life to identify the root causes of many of the issues and pain that I have experienced. Meeting her was one of the biggest blessings ever, and I must credit her with much of my growth. As I've said, most of what I talk about in this book are only things I became aware of after working with her.

ʃ

Since learning more about depression and how it can present itself, it has become clear to me that I was depressed way before the events of 2016, particularly during my time in India. I was just completely unaware that what I was going through was depression.

As I've said, when I was in India, I was in a place where I didn't want to be, in an environment that I was not cut out for and, for the majority of the time, doing something I didn't enjoy. I was miserable. However, if someone had told me then that I could have been depressed, I would have laughed at the mere suggestion. That's because I had an idea in my head of what depression should look like and I certainly didn't fit that framework. One of the most important lessons I've learnt from the self-work experience is not to have any judgements about the way things 'should' look, or how things 'should' feel. For example, if you have preconceived notions the way I did of what depression 'should look like', or what anxiety 'should feel like', you can end up missing what's right in front of you. I see now that things such as the drinking and the partying were often done to mask the depression I was feeling, although at the time I would not have put the two together.

The most important bit of advice I could give you from my experience is don't feel afraid to seek help. And don't ever feel guilty for what you feel. You would not think twice about going to a doctor if you were feeling unwell, so if you're not feeling all good upstairs, speak to a professional. There's absolutely no shame in it and it's certainly not weakness. In fact, saying, 'I need help', is a big show of strength.

People have asked me, when is it time to seek help? I've asked my therapist this question and it seems the general thinking is if the symptoms go on for more than a couple of weeks, you should speak to a professional. I know access to professionals isn't the same for everyone. So if you can't see a psychiatrist or psychologist, try and see your doctor, because they can also set you up with medication and other things to get you going. There are also many resources online. Whatever you choose to do, the sooner you seek help the better.

That's my story with depression, and while it did take a toll on me, I do feel that a lot of benefits came out of my experience. First, it made me take a deeper look at myself, which served as the catalyst to my self-work journey. Second, it taught me that it's okay to be vulnerable and to seek help. It took me a long time to learn this, but allowing myself to be vulnerable has been the most liberating thing ever. And third, it helped me see that we shouldn't have preconceived notions about how something 'should' look.

In my acting studio in LA, maybe a year and a half ago, I was given an exercise to draw the best day and the worst day of my life. For the worst day of my life, I drew a picture from the day I sat on the stairs, crying in front of the mirror, feeling I had a dementor on my shoulder. If I were given the same exercise today, I would probably draw the same picture as the best day of my life. Because that was the day I finally decided to put my guard down. That day was the start of my journey of self-work and spirituality that has formed the basis of my life ever since.

three

The Force of Divorce

Divorce is one of those things that I don't think gets the importance it should in discussions of mental health. Maybe because it's so common that people just accept it as an 'unfortunate event' without paying much attention to the repercussions it can have on the physical, emotional and mental health of those concerned. But those who have either experienced divorce themselves or who have divorced parents know what a traumatic experience it can be. As with all traumatic events, the residue stays with you long after the event has passed. For me, issues such as loneliness and feelings of abandonment stemmed off the back of my parents' divorce.

The experiences and events I talk about in this chapter, particularly with regard to my dad's other family, are those between the ages of nine, when I first met them, to around twenty-one. After that, I didn't have much contact with them since my dad's relationship with my stepmother took a different turn. Recently, though, I have reconnected with my half-sisters, as we are all older now and have lives of our own. I'll start by walking you through how I remember the divorce unfolding, how it affected me and the issues I faced off the back of it.

✗

I have lots of memories of the time that my parents were together. As a child, I was very fortunate I got to travel the world with them and experience many things. My dad was not always around, though, because he was in India or elsewhere working (or doing other things I found out about later!), and I remember the excitement I always felt when he came into town. We lived in a huge house and for the majority of the time it was just my mom, my grandmother (dad's mom) and myself, and at times the house could feel quite empty. But when my dad was there, the whole house would come alive and had a kind of energy it didn't otherwise have.

We also had a second home near Southampton on the south coast of England, and my mom, my dad, me and a bunch of my parents' friends would go there on weekend trips. I loved it because we were all together.

Then I remember going on a couple of trips where it was just my dad and me. One of those was to South Africa, which was a great place to go as a kid. Being in the African bush, going on safari and seeing all the amazing animals in the wild were experiences that I absolutely loved. At the time, I didn't really question why my mom wasn't there, and I guess I saw those trips as father-son holidays. Either that or I was so caught up in the excitement that it probably didn't even register to me that she was absent! It certainly wouldn't have crossed my mind that perhaps the reason my mom wasn't there was because there might have been issues between the two of them.

The next distinct thing I remember was my dad showing me photographs of two little girls. One was a toddler named Leana and the other was a newborn named Tanya. He told me these two girls were my sisters. I don't think I fully comprehended what that meant at the time. After all, I was eight years old, so what is one really meant to think or say? I do know though that my mom was upset that my dad had told me about them without her being there because she has since said that she had wanted them to tell me together. Obviously my mom was well aware of my dad's new family long before I was. Oh, and just for good measure, let me tell you that the woman who was now my dad's wife used to be a friend of my mom's. How's that for Shakespearian drama?

Of course when you're that young, you don't really think twice about this kind of thing or appreciate the possible implications of finding out that you actually share your parent with two other people and the effect it can have on your psyche. So I just went along with it all.

Two other moments during this time stick out for me as well. The first was finding a book in my mom's room that was titled something like 'How to Deal with Divorce'. At first my mom sort of brushed it off when I asked her about it. Then she said she had bought that book for me to find and read.

The second was that I had to go to court. I was in year four at school at the time and thought it was great because it meant I could miss a day of school. When you are that young, any excuse to get a day off from school is a win, even if it means going to court because your parents are going to divorce! Looking back now, not only does it seem absurd to drag a child to court, but it also may well have been one of the things that triggered my irrational fear of going to jail. (I talk about this in my chapter on drinking.) In court, I was taken into a room without my parents. A lady who must have been one of the attorneys asked if I was aware that my dad had a new partner. Now, I knew about my stepmother at this point, but I said, 'No, I don't know.' The lady looked a little confused by my answer. After all, that's why I was in the court, right? But it turned out that I was the one who was confused. I thought the word 'partner' meant business partner, not 'significant other'! Oh, the innocence of youth!

For years, I couldn't understand why on earth I was dragged to court that day. Only when I started writing this book did I ask my mom about it. She told me that my dad had wanted me for half the school holidays, but she was apprehensive about me meeting my dad's new family. It was, therefore, decided that I should be the one who got to choose. No pressure for a nine-year-old! Whilst I still think that taking a nine-year-old to court is not the smartest thing in the world to do, I do understand that it was done to protect me and my interests. As the saying goes, 'Everyone has their day in court.' I guess mine just came a little sooner than most!

ſ

The point when it all truly became real was when I was finally introduced to my dad's new family. It was Christmas day, 1996 (my dad had got his wish; I was spending half the holidays with him). I knew I had two half-sisters, but I don't recall being told prior to this trip that my dad's new wife (my stepmother as she now was) also had two children from her previous marriage—a boy and a girl who were about my age, and who my dad had effectively embraced as his own. When we arrived in the airport, I saw a boy who looked around my age walking towards us, waving his hand at my dad. I asked who that was and he said it was my stepmother's son. I thought, 'What a cool guy!' He was dressed well, he had a backpack on and, compared to him, I looked like a total dork.

When we got to where we were staying, I was introduced to my stepmother, my stepsister (my stepmom's daughter from her previous marriage) and also my half-sister who was my dad's daughter. I know all this 'step' and 'half' lingo might be hard to keep up with. Trust me, it took me a while to figure out who I was actually related to and who I wasn't! After the introductions were made, my stepmom asked if I was okay sharing a room with her son. I remember thinking, 'Yeah, absolutely! It's gonna be like a two-week sleepover.' I was so excited by all these new people in my life, thinking how cool it was to have a family that was more than just my parents and me. And when I returned home to my mom in England, it was a huge comedown from the excitement and novelty of what I had just experienced.

It was really only after I started working with my therapist that I started to acknowledge what a big deal it was to meet this new family on that trip. To suddenly have so many new people thrust in my life all in one go was definitely a shock to my system. That coupled with the fact that they all existed without my knowledge has been something that has caused me much mental anguish over the years. It's only in the last few years that I have been able to really see how this affected me and been able to process it.

ʃ

One of the issues I've struggled with through my life that I can link back to the divorce is loneliness. Up until a couple of years ago if somebody had asked me what my biggest fear was, I would've said loneliness. (Sharks would have come a close second!) I can pinpoint exactly when loneliness started to become an issue for me. It was upon my return from my first trip to meet my dad's new family, when I literally went from being an only child to one of five overnight (if you include my stepmother's two kids from her previous marriage).

I remember coming back to my mom from that trip and going into my bedroom. Even though nothing had physically changed, it felt as though everything had changed. I felt an emptiness in the room; everything looked grey and gloomy, like there was this dark filter over my eyes. I also felt an emptiness inside. Almost as if I had lost something. So I sat on the floor with some colouring pencils and paper and drew pictures of me with my new family to remember them. (I think I'd seen some kid do this in a film once.) That was the first time in my life I believe I was aware that I was lonely. Because to fully appreciate anything in life, you need to experience the opposite. For me loneliness didn't exist until I had experienced companionship. And companionship is exactly what I had during that trip. Now that I was no longer with my new family, I knew what it really felt like to be on my own.

I often joke that I went on that trip as an only child and came back as a lonely child.

ʄ

Moving forwards, I had to split the school holidays between my mom and my dad until I was eighteen. This arrangement is pretty standard for kids from divorce. But living two separate lives with two different families further contributed to my feelings of loneliness and instability.

The four other children (my two half-sisters and my stepbrother and stepsister) all had the same mother, so they lived together. They were based on the west coast of America. On the other hand, I lived with my mom in the UK and would only see them during the school holidays three or four times a year for a couple of weeks to a month at a time, depending how long the holidays were. Every time one of those trips came up, I'd be super excited. On the flip side, at the end of the trip, I'd be crushed. On the flight back home, knowing that all the other kids got to stay together, I'd feel alone and abandoned. I used to beg my dad at the end of every trip to go to court and get full custody of me, so I could live with him and them.

This constant coming and going had me crying myself to sleep many a night under the bed covers in our big dorm room at boarding school. I would literally have to bite on the duvet to muffle the sound, so the other kids wouldn't wake up. That's how much of an impact it had on me every time I had to leave that other family. I just felt alone.

While for the most part I enjoyed being with my dad's new family, there was a part of me that also felt like an outsider when I was with them. All those kids lived together with their mother, but I was just sporadically coming and going, so sometimes I felt as though I was on the outside looking in. Often, when they talked about school or other things, I'd have no clue what they were talking about. I'd just sit there, trying my hardest to chime in, wishing I could be a part of the discussion. I once saw a picture up on the wall in the house. One of my sisters had drawn it at school. It was titled 'My Family', and there were stick figures of her, our dad, her mom and her three other siblings—everyone but me. I don't think I was intentionally left out, but because I wasn't constantly there like her other siblings, she didn't feel a connection to me. Seeing that picture was heart-breaking. Things like that made me feel like a total outsider, not part of the family. And even though I was physically with them, I could sometimes still feel I was on my own.

My stepmom had a big hand in making me feel this way as well. She could sometimes be the sweetest, kindest, most caring person in the world. She could make me feel like I was her own, no different than her biological children. On one occasion I overheard her speaking to some friends and telling them she had five kids. Obviously she was referring to the four of her own and me, and I remember how much joy I felt hearing that because I felt accepted and acknowledged. But as sweet and as kind and as caring as she could be, she was more often than not a very cold person who could make me feel unloved, unappreciated and, worst of all, unwanted.

I've heard stories about her and the way she used to badmouth my mom and me to my dad. I was once told that one of the things she had told him was that I was sly. As a child, there were a number of adjectives that could have been used to describe me, but sly was definitely not one of them! Partly because I was just too innocent and partly because I was a very naïve and easily manipulated kid who couldn't tell a lie for love or money! My mom always said, 'The one thing Sidhartha can't do is lie!' But even though I would feel the pain of my stepmother's rejection, I would cling to the love she sporadically gave me, and as a result, I would bury the pain of feeling like an outsider.

My stepmother and I recently talked about all of this. To her credit, she offered me an apology for everything she put me through. She admitted to me that often it wasn't anger towards me, but misdirected anger she had towards my dad. Why she had anger towards him, I don't know. What I do know is that she took out her emotions on me! This 'misdirected' anger was very prevalent when I was a child, but I believe in moving on and in accepting an apology when it is offered. Does that mean we are best buds now? Of course not, and nor do we have to be. But I will always respect that she is the mother of my two half-sisters, so I will always be open to making the relationship work for their sake.

ʃ

This longing to be part of a family and the longing for some sort of stability is something I've dealt with throughout my life. I realise that it has shown up the most in my relationships. I've had four serious girlfriends and while each of them has been a wonderful, beautiful human being in her own right, they had one thing in common. They all came from super secure and tightknit families, with multiple siblings, cousins, etc., who all supported one another. Whenever I was with my girlfriends and their families, I felt the same joy as I first had when I met my dad's new family. All the girls' families were super sweet and nice to me and seeing the love they shared filled me with happiness, comfort and, most important, hope.

When your parents divorce, you can really go one of two ways. Either you become apprehensive of marriage and having a family of your own because you saw what happened to your parents and how you suffered, or you really crave it because you want the stability you never had. For me it has certainly been the latter. I used to joke with one of my girlfriends that I wanted seven children, like the Von Trapp family in *The Sound of Music*. She said that if I was willing to go through the process of childbirth myself, I could have as many kids as I wanted, but since she would have to do the hard work, it was four maximum. Fair point. (Although she did say we could have three dogs to take the total to seven, so it was a more than fair compromise!)

Stability and family are big parts of what attracts me to someone. My best friend growing up also came from a very close-knit family. He used to tell me about their family tradition every Christmas of waking up, having breakfast and opening presents all together. I always said I loved hearing about things like that; that I really wished I could do that one day with a family. And he always laughed whenever I said that and say he wished he could have my life because I got to travel and so on. He thought my life was great and could never understand why I would want what he had. A lot of people who come from close-knit families don't understand that those of us who don't have them can crave them. No matter how many material possessions you have, they can never compare to the stability and security that family can offer.

Another area where my issues with loneliness came up was when I used to drink. I always wanted to continue the party till the early hours of the morning; I never wanted the night to end. That's because when I was out with friends, I felt I was a part of something. I felt companionship. The end of the night, on the other hand, signified going back to being alone.

On one occasion, a friend of mine and I were at a party that finished around 3 a.m. We then went to an after-party that ended around 6 a.m. At this point, we were both totally boozed up and it was probably a good indication that we should hit the hay. However, when we got back home, I convinced him to sit on the rooftop and continue drinking. I told him we should do it to watch the sunrise, but if I'm honest it was really because I didn't want the night to end and I didn't want to feel alone.

I tried to avoid these lonely feelings as much as possible, looking for stability, family and community in whatever I could. When I lived in India, I worked for the Royal Challengers Bangalore cricket team that participated in the Indian Premier League and I loved the experience. Many people think that's because of the parties and the glitz and the glamour that came with being part of the league. But in reality it was because for those seven weeks that the league played, I lived and travelled with the team and it made me feel part of something. We were a family.

This is also one of the big things that attracted me to acting. Apart from the opportunity to express myself creatively, acting gives me the opportunity to be a part of something. When I shot my first film, *Brahman Naman*, being on set was the best experience ever. Here was this group of artistes all working together for a common goal. It was a family.

✗

So far this chapter has focused on my relationships and experiences with my new family. But what about the relationships I shared with my parents after divorce? Let's start with my old man. Our relationship over the years has been a rollercoaster of emotions for both of us.

My dad was my hero when I was a child. The fun we had together was legendary. I was a very playful child and he was a very playful adult. But after the divorce, I felt as though I had lost him to his new family. I started seeing him less than I already did and, whether he intended it or not, his daughters seemed to become his priority. I'm not sure if this is just something that happens when a man has a new family, but I felt as though I had been replaced. I also felt a change in his behaviour towards me. He used to get very irritable with me, which was something he'd never done before. At times I felt I'd become an inconvenience to him. I don't know if what my stepmother had said to him about me was having an effect, but I saw and felt him shift. Nonetheless, I loved him and loved the time I was with him as well.

Then in my twenties, my feelings towards my dad started to change. My emotions from the divorce that had been unconsciously bottled up for many years started to bubble up to the surface. Now that I was a lot older, I felt things differently than I had when I was a child. A lot of what I felt was anger and, because at that point I hadn't done the self-work I have today, it made me very bitter and resentful towards him.

The fact that he had had another family without my knowledge when I'd thought I was his only child started to play on my mind. For the first time I started to feel as though I had been lied to and cheated. This was something I carried around with me until quite recently.

After I explored this with my therapist a few years ago, I learnt that these feelings were because I had felt as though I had been abandoned by him.

Today he talks about how he used to commute between India and the United States because the elder of his two daughters made him promise he would come and see her as much as he could. While I think it's amazing that he did that for her, I can't help but feel a bit bad every time I hear it because the time he spent with his new family was time he hadn't spent with me.

In terms of lifestyle and all that sort of stuff, I was very well looked after my whole life. I got to go on great holidays, I attended the best schools, had new clothes and so on. From a material point of view, I had everything any child could ever want, and my dad provided above and beyond what any parent had to. But I came to realise that what I had always craved the most was love and emotional support from him. I think I had it at times when I was a child, but at other times I didn't feel I had it at all, especially after the divorce.

I remember when I was about eleven or twelve years old I was playing in a cricket match at my prep school. My dad happened to be in the UK and surprised me by coming to watch the game. Most of the other kids would have their moms and dads come every week to watch them play sport, and while my mom was a constant at all my school matches, my dad was never there. So having him there that day was special. (If I remember correctly, I hit my highest score of the season that match as well!) I think my happiness was in part because my father was there, but partly also because, somewhere in me, I felt reassured that he still valued me despite having another family. It may have taken me a long time to realise this, but I valued moments like this so much more than anything material I was given.

About a year and a half ago, I had a big discussion with my dad where I pretty much unloaded everything I had been feeling for the past twenty years. I had so many things I wanted to say to him and ask him about, and I finally felt like I was in the right place to do so, having done all my self-work. One of the things we spoke about was the divorce. I told him how I felt about the fact he had had another family without my knowledge. His response to this was to (quite rightly) ask: what would have been the right way to tell me?

The truth is, I don't know. I don't know if there is any 'right way' to handle this sort of situation. My dad himself is an only child of divorced parents. His father also had another family. I'm sure he suffered as well. So I'm sure he just did what he thought was right based on his own experiences. I think often we can forget that our parents also had their own childhoods and experienced things that can influence the way they are as adults. I don't think this was a point I fully comprehended until very recently.

During this chat I also mentioned how I had felt as though he wasn't there for me after the divorce.

His response to this was that he had never felt he had mistreated me and that he had always provided for me through my life. I told him that from a material point of view that was certainly true, but what I missed was the emotional providing. This was something he didn't seem to understand. For all the great qualities he possesses, one thing I feel my dad has lacked in life is empathy and this certainly seemed to show here. He just didn't seem to understand where I was coming from. All he could see was the material side of things. This was very disappointing and frustrating for me because there was still a part of me that was looking for an emotional connection from him to come through.

About six months before I started writing this book, I mentioned this to someone and they gave me a way of looking at it I hadn't considered before. They said that for most Indian fathers, the belief is that their job is to provide for their family financially. The emotional side is the mom's job. I'm not sure if this is true for everyone, and I would hate to generalise, but I found this quite interesting, and thought perhaps this is why my dad couldn't see where I was coming from. While I still think there is a disconnect between us in terms of what we value, I do at least have a different lens through which to view his actions.

All in all, what I have come to realise and accept through my self-work is that I don't think he ever went out of his way to cause me the distress that I've felt. Sometimes you can be very unaware of how your actions can affect others and I think this was the case with my dad. I still might not agree with everything he did, but I've learnt to accept it and accept him. Today I am very clear on who he is and he is very clear on who I am, what he values and what I value, what his beliefs are and what my beliefs are. What his personality is, and what my personality is. And how all that differs between us. At the end of the long chat, we came to the conclusion that we were just very different people at this stage in our lives. And that was completely okay. He also made it clear that at his age, he is not going to change! So will I ever have a close emotional bond with my dad? Maybe not. But I am now able to accept it and move on in peace without holding on to resentments or expectations of what I wanted him to be while I was growing up.

One thing I want to mention on this point above is that it's important to recognise and accept that people are different, and that is totally okay—even if you are related to them by blood. A question I got asked a lot after doing the ConSIDer This series was how to deal with family members you might not align with. My response was always that it was okay not to align! I think there can sometimes be a belief that we must always get on with and understand members of our family. But at the end of the day, be it

a brother, father, daughter, mother, cousin, aunt, etc.,
everyone is an individual with different personalities,
beliefs and values. It's unlikely that everyone is going
to have everything in common with everyone else.
Also, we should remember that people change and
grow. Just because you were close to someone at
one stage doesn't mean that you will remain so
forever. People drift apart. It's a part of life. Most
of the time, there isn't even an inciting incident that
makes people go their separate ways; it's just that
where those two people are in their lives might not
necessarily align anymore. That doesn't mean they
have to become enemies though. How many times
have we had super close friendships that have just
drifted apart? It happens all the time. And this can
be said for family as well. I know there are those
who might not agree with what I'm saying here; they
will say that family is everything. I agree with the
importance of having a strong family bond. As I've
said throughout this chapter, being a part of a family
is something I've craved, but at the same time, I also
believe in the importance of being your own person.

I would say that the realisations my dad and
I came to are very healthy because we now see
and accept that we are very different and are on
very different paths. We understand the fundamental
differences between us and can, therefore, have a
relationship based on mutual respect, as opposed to
one of us either changing ourselves to fit with the

other person, or trying to change the other person to fit in line with us.

✺

Now for my mom…

About six months after I met my dad's new family, my mom and I had to move out of our house because the divorce had been finalised. This hit me hard. I found it difficult to adjust to the change in environment, going from the house where I had grown up to a new place where it was now just the two of us. The home we moved to was a lovely one not too far from where we had been living, but psychologically, I don't think either of us was prepared or equipped to deal with the change. I certainly wasn't. I was only ten.

My behaviour became especially aggressive during this time. For the most part, I was a very playful child, but I did have a lot of anger inside me, as well as a very short temper. Anger is something that many children who come from some sort of instability deal with while growing up, even if they aren't aware that the instability is causing the anger. As it was now just my mom and me, I would take most of my anger out on her. I wished more than anything back then that I could go and live with my dad's other family and I used to think that my mom was the reason I couldn't; that she was an evil person holding me back from them. I used to shout at her, I used to break stuff and say things, such as how I preferred my dad and how I would rather live with him and his family. Pretty horrible stuff.

My mom, seeing the pain I was in and being the kind soul she is, took it for the most part. But being only human herself, she occasionally retaliated and said negative things about my dad, stepmom and my half-sisters to me. I thought she was just an awful person for saying those sorts of things about them. I didn't realise at the time that she was dealing with her own pain—the pain these people had caused her. When you are young, seeing an adult, especially a parent, act out is very jarring and this made me act out even more.

She also started seeing another man at this time as well, whom she is still with today. He was someone I actually knew quite well because, wait for it, he used to work for my dad! In hindsight this is something that I found difficult to take at the time. For years I was very embarrassed by my mom's new relationship. At school, when I was asked how he and my mom met, I used to deflect the subject because I didn't want to say he was an ex-employee. And I think this just added to the anger I was already feeling.

Since his tenure as an employee of my dad had ended in rather negative circumstances, he carried bitterness and resentment towards my dad himself.

So when I would get angry and shout at him (because of my own bitterness and anger towards all the sudden changes), he'd say negative things back to me about my dad. At that time I thought he was an awful human being as well for saying the things he said, but of course now I see that it was another example of 'misdirected anger'. I will say, though, that the support he provided my mom through the years has been fantastic. When I was young, I didn't appreciate what he was doing for my mother, but as I grew up I came to see the positive impact he had. For that I will always be grateful to him.

Finally, there were also people from my dad's side who would make comments about my mom. One of his employees talked about the money my mom took in the divorce as if she had somehow looted my dad. It was money she was entitled to, but at the time I was too young to understand this, so comments like that added to the image I had of her as being an awful person.

All in all, the relationship I had with my mother was filled with lots of anger and acting out, predominantly from my side. All this was based on the false image I had of her, and the pain I was experiencing, due to the vast amounts of change that were happening all at once around me.

As the years went on, and I finally grew up, I started to see that my mother was never the awful monster I had thought she was, but in fact the complete opposite. She was a loving, caring human being trying her level best to look after her son. She always put my emotional needs first, and even though she may not at times have known how to handle me, she always tried her best. After working with my therapist and digging deeper into the feelings that stemmed from the divorce, I came to learn that the anger I had towards my mother was my own misdirected anger, anger that had developed from feeling abandoned, cheated and let down by my dad. A couple of years ago, after I made all these discoveries in therapy, I called my mom and apologised for my behaviour during my youth. She said I had nothing to be sorry for; that she had always known that the anger and pain I took out on her had never actually been aimed at her.

Since doing my self-work, I have developed a new-found level of respect for my mom. For a child, it's natural to only think about yourself without consideration for your parents. Children see adults as superhero-like figures that provide comfort and safety. They tend not to think of their parents as human too. This was what I did with respect to my mother. After all, here was this young woman from a middle-class Muslim family. She got married. She moved countries. She had a child. And then everything around her fell apart. What I've really come to appreciate is that this happened when she wasn't very many years older than I am today. I never appreciated what the situation was like for her. She had to handle her own pain in the best way she knew how, while at the same time trying to look after the well-being of her child. I will always love my mom and respect her for the way she tried her best.

After I started my advocacy around mental health, my mom and I have spoken about the divorce and our experiences at length. One thing we agree on is that we both could have used some sort of professional help or guidance during that time. After all, we had both been thrust into a situation that neither of us had been prepared for and we had both been holding on to anger, pain and a world of emotion that neither of us was equipped to deal with or knew how to process. Today we laugh about it because it was a case of the blind leading the blind: two people trying to figure things out as they went along. Back then though, mental health wasn't really given much importance, so I don't think it would have crossed anyone's mind that both parent and child could have benefitted from professional help.

∫

The divorce caused me a lot of pain throughout my life. However, there is always light to be found in even the darkest of times, and since working through the divorce with my therapist, I have been able to find some positives and learnings from the experience.

First, I'm very happy that I didn't live with the other family! As much as I said I wanted to, I now see that it was just my emotions talking. Had I gone, it would have been the wrong thing for me and the wrong thing to do to my mom. Changing environments and growing up with another family without my mother would have caused me even more psychological issues than they would have solved!

Second, the divorce showed me the sort of person/ husband/father I want to be and what I don't want to be if I'm one day fortunate enough to have a family of my own. That close-knit bond where everybody feels supported and loved is something I will strive to ensure for my family. I will continue to do whatever self-work is necessary to fully process any pain I still hold on to from my own experience of coming from divorce, so that I don't carry any of that baggage into my own relationship and family. In order to be the best possible husband / father / wife / mother / sibling / friend and so on, I think we each need to get our own house in order first.

This leads to the next learning, which is the importance of processing one's anger. As I said, growing up there was so much misdirected anger around me from people who were carrying their own pain. I experienced both sides of this. Having the misdirected anger. And receiving it. There was my stepmom who would direct her anger at me, even though it was my father she was upset with. My grandmother used to have anger towards just about everyone, but that was largely because she was holding on to her own pain from her divorce from forty years before. My mom and her partner used to badmouth my dad to me, which of course was their own anger aimed at him. And finally there was me, taking out all my emotions on my mom, when really the anger I had was towards the situation in general. (Side note here. My dad was the only one who NEVER said a bad word about my mom to me ever, and for that I will always respect him.)

What I have learnt from this is how important it is to work through our issues and allow ourselves time to process and heal from the pain we have experienced. Otherwise what can end up happening is that you can carry the anger, and the fears, insecurities, judgements, resentments, etc., into everything else you do in life, and take it out on the wrong person.

The divorce also taught me to look for the best in everyone and to be compassionate. People we interact with carry their own unprocessed emotional baggage which can be projected onto us and can make us act out towards them. For example, my dad. I don't think my dad intentionally caused pain to anyone. He just might be carrying his own unprocessed feelings from his childhood with him still, which may come out in ways he's not even aware of. So there is no point reacting to him with resentment or anger. Learning to treat him with compassion and love instead of bitterness and resentment not only helped bring out the best in me, but also brought out a softer side in him.

Finally, by exploring the divorce in depth, I have been able to let go of my feelings of loneliness. I learnt that what I needed to do was to get comfortable with myself, especially when I was on my own. Two things really helped me with this. First, meditation. Meditation trained me to find an inner peace and to just sit on my own with that peace. Second, books like *The Power of Now* by Eckhart Tolle taught me to get more in tune with myself. One of the big things *The Power of Now* taught me is that you are never really alone because you are always with yourself. This was a huge discovery for me, and today I no longer look to others to fill a void because I feel as though I have everything I need within myself to feel complete and whole.

So if you suffer from loneliness, spend time getting comfortable with yourself. Spend time befriending yourself. I know this sounds like New Age craziness, and I probably thought that as well when I first started doing it. But it's really not. There are those who, over the past year, have spent the coronavirus-enforced lockdown with their entire family and still felt very alone. There are others who have been in lockdown by themselves and felt completely at peace. I fell into the latter category and that's because of the work I did getting comfortable with myself.

ʃ

The divorce shaped so much of my life. Some good things came out of it and some not so great things. Either way, it had a lasting psychological impact on me and only after taking a deep dive into my past with my therapist did I come to fully appreciate the impact of it all and just how much bitterness, resentment and pain I had been holding on to for so many years.

A divorce and its aftermath can be a seriously traumatic event and, because of this, I feel it's vital that people are given the emotional and mental support they need. I would therefore implore anyone who might be going through a divorce to please get the psychological advice and guidance you need in order to deal with your situation—parents and children alike!

four

Lose the Booze

It took me a long time to realise the impact alcohol was having on my life. It was only after really getting to know myself that I came to see it. Alcohol has affected me in a number of different ways at different stages of my life. Because I didn't see the issues as they happened, they had a knock-on effect until I got to the point of realisation.

I want to make clear before I go on that I was never an alcoholic. I was never dependent on it. But that doesn't mean that alcohol didn't have a negative effect on me. If there is one takeaway from this chapter, let it be this: You don't have to be an actual alcoholic for drinking to be bad for you and your mental health. Like I mentioned in the chapter on depression, we often have a framework of how something should look before we classify it as either a problem or something we need to address. And in this chapter, I will share how you don't need to be a drunk or even reliant on alcohol for it to have a negative effect on your life and mental well-being.

ʃ

My family was one of the biggest producers of alcohol in the world. So I grew up around alcohol and even worked in the alcohol industry before going into entertainment. The company was started by my grandfather and it was taken on and grown by my dad. So let's address an important question that I'm sure you might have: 'Why is a guy who comes from a family that produces alcohol writing a chapter about not drinking?'

Here's why.

On 6 August 2018, I decided to stop drinking. I didn't say for how long I was going to stop. I just decided that at that point in time, alcohol was having more of a negative effect than a positive one on me, so until I got myself in order, I was going to take a break.

On the one-year anniversary of the day I stopped, I put up a brief Instagram story explaining why I had decided to stop and that it had been a year since I'd last had a drink. And I was flooded with messages from people who said they could relate with my issues and with my story. A lot of them went on to ask for advice.

What struck me the most was how many of them said that by hearing my admission, they themselves felt inspired to stop or control their drinking— something they previously might not have felt they could do—because if a person from an alcohol-producing family could make the change, then they could as well.

That's why I felt compelled to do an entire episode on this in my ConSIDer This series and also to include a chapter on it in this book.

Before I continue, I want to say that I don't think alcohol is bad. (I've had some legendary experiences where alcohol has been involved!) But it becomes bad or has a negative effect on you when it starts to get in the way of other parts of your life, such as your profession, your relationships and your mental well-being. Something that happened to me.

∫

The first time I ever got drunk was when I was eleven. Completely by accident. My best friend had a brother a couple of years older than us who was a very good rugby player. He went on to have a very successful international career as well. At that time, his team had qualified for the National Schools Championship to be played at the National Rugby Stadium, Twickenham, in London. So his parents organised a mini bus to take friends and family to watch the game and I was invited along. On that bus, beers were being handed around and some of the older kids were drinking them. Somehow, a couple of these beverages ended up in my hand. Not wanting to look a fool or to be the odd one out, I decided to partake in the libation. At this point in my life, all I knew about beer was that it was an orangey colour drink that my dad's company produced. I took my first sip of it and wanted to puke straight away. It was the most disgusting thing I had ever tasted and I wondered to myself how on earth my dad made a living from selling this shit and why people would buy it. Nonetheless, I powered through and I finished a can and a half. The next day I woke up with the worst headache I have ever had. It was the school holidays and a teacher had come to give me maths tuition. I was already useless at maths when I was sober, and my hungover state only made me worse. I remember in the middle of it having to go to the toilet and throw up.

So that was my first experience of getting 'drunk' and experiencing the physical effects alcohol can have on the system. I know several kids 'accidentally' get drunk and the experience of puking their guts out can put them off alcohol for life. Looking back, I wish that experience had, at the very least, made me more cautious of alcohol, but it certainly didn't!

It was at the age of fourteen at Wellington that I properly started to experience 'drinking'. It was just part of the culture at boarding school back then. Were we getting paralytically drunk? No. Were we sneaking off into the bushes with a brightly coloured alcopop and thinking we were the coolest kids in the world? Yes.

We relied on one friend who, let's say, was a little more confident than the rest, to get the sauce for us. On one occasion, he had with him at school an extra set of his uncle's car keys. I have no clue why. So when we needed alcohol, he ran into the off-licence, threw the keys down on the counter, pointed to them and yelled to the shop attendant, 'My wife is out in the car in labour', and that he immediately needed a six pack of beer and some Smirnoff Ices. The guy probably went into such shock at the sight of this kid shouting at him that he lost any sense of rational perception and gave my friend the booze without question. That was the kind of antics we'd perform to get our alcohol. Either that or buy it from some of the older kids in our boarding house. And the thrill of actually getting it was way more exciting than the drinking of it.

The school itself would provide alcohol for us on certain occasions. For example, at our boarding house Christmas dinner every year, there would be wine freely available for all the kids, regardless of age. And in my last year at the school, we had something known as the 'JCR' or 'Junior Common Room'. In its simplest description, the JCR was a bar. It served beer and wine three times a week, and students in what was known as the upper sixth form (12th standard) would be allowed to go there and have up to two drinks. JCRs were very common in British public schools back then, but I believe a law was passed soon after I left, which meant schools could no longer operate them. I think the reason for both the JCR and the alcohol at certain school functions was to teach us from a young age to appreciate alcohol and learn moderation. After all, the more you keep something away from someone, the more they are likely to want it. As you will see, this logic didn't work with me!

I would also drink when I went to India in the summer holidays. We used to go out in Bangalore and get, to use an appropriate term for the time, 'wasted'. The only way to get into the venues was to bribe the bouncer at the door because we were underage. This only added to the excitement and the thrill. The drink of choice would either be some sort of fluorescent shot that had more chance of giving you diabetes than getting you drunk, or B52s. The sheer memory of them makes me want to throw up!

Now I'm not condoning the behaviour I've written about so far, but to me it was all just harmless fun at the time and no one was getting hurt. If you had asked me back then what my thoughts on alcohol were, I would have instantly said it was associated with fun and having a good time. If you had asked me what the dangers or effects of alcohol could be, I would have said it could cause liver damage. If you had asked me at what point alcohol becomes problematic, I would have said only when you became an alcoholic. Basically, all my answers would have been in line with what we are taught about alcohol, which focused pretty much exclusively on its physical effects.

At no point then would I have even considered the mental effects it could have. In no way would I have been able to comprehend how it could be bad for someone who wasn't an alcoholic. So I really didn't see much of a downside to it. In fact, I always thought smoking was much worse. At boarding school, the smoking culture was huge—many of the kids between the ages of thirteen and eighteen smoked. I always believed that smoking could cause much worse problems than drinking could, and that's why I stayed away from it; even to this day, I've never had a puff of a cigarette.

So far what I've mentioned doesn't seem much of a problem, right? It's part of being young and of growing up. So why do I tell you all this then? Well, first just to share a few anecdotes from my past that might make you giggle. But also to highlight that it was a time when I was completely unaware of the full impact that alcohol could have.

After I left Wellington at eighteen and went to university, the drinking was taken to a whole new level. It was at university that I probably first encountered the negative side of alcohol. Suddenly I wasn't on a strict regimen anymore and I could do pretty much whatever I wanted, whenever I wanted. (Oh and I was finally of the legal drinking age as well!) This more often than not resulted in me going to the Students Union and getting on the beers instead of attending my business management seminars. I remember the exchange students who would come over from the US for a semester would get absolutely hammered on every occasion they could because the drinking age in the UK was eighteen. (Back in the US, it was twenty-one.) I used to laugh because they behaved like they had never seen alcohol before. But in hindsight, if I'm honest, I was no better!

For the three years I was at Queen Mary, I was probably drunk 75 per cent of the time. I was captain of the men's hockey team and by my third year, I was also the chairman of the club. For those of you who know anything about British societies or sports clubs at universities, there is a massive drinking culture. The amount of booze I drank definitely exceeded the amount of hockey I played. The boozing went on at all hours. For example, we would take gin and tonics into our lectures, disguised in coffee mugs. Assuming I even went to a lecture. The drinking certainly got in the way of my studies, either because I was missing lectures to get on the sauce or because I was too hungover to attend them. That's why I say it was having a negative effect on me: it was getting in the way of what I was actually there to do. By the end of my time at Queen Mary, I hadn't learnt much about business, but had definitely learnt everything there was to know about drinking games and drinking songs.

The way we drank was relentless. It would never just be one or two pints. Pretty much every time I got on it, it would turn into a full-blown bender. I had zero concept of moderation or balance back then, and this probably had the most lasting effect on me from the time. It shaped the way I drank from then on. It was always all or nothing.

I still struggle with balance today. I am still quite extreme. I have great willpower and can hold myself back from giving into pretty much any craving, but once I start something, I go all in. This happens with food, with work, with working out. And while there are merits to going all in, in certain aspects I've recently learnt the importance of finding the middle ground. Maybe if I had learnt balance and moderation back then with regard to drinking, I would be better positioned today in other areas of my life. At university you are at an age when your behaviour can have an impact on your life moving forwards. But I didn't see that. I just saw myself as a kid who was having fun.

I also had no sense of my limits. I could drink a lot! But because I never threw up or passed out, I would just keep going on and on. I would think I was okay because I was still standing, but to everyone else, I was a mess. This could at times make me not the most pleasant of drunks. I had quite a mouth on me, and this caused me to get into a number of altercations. I purposely use the word 'altercation' instead of 'fight', because most of the time it would just be drunken youths mouthing off to each other without any punches thrown. Having said that, on one occasion I was hit on the head with a glass cider bottle, which resulted in me being taken away in an ambulance to get my head stitched up.

Overall, during my time at university, I had no sense of knowing where to draw the line. I was compulsive, aggressive and extreme with regard to my relationship to alcohol.

But I did still manage to graduate with a top degree. Perhaps this subconsciously made me feel that the way I was drinking wasn't a problem.

When I graduated from Queen Mary and started work at the global drinks company, Diageo, my mindset was still very much that of a student. And my behaviour with regard to alcohol reflected that. If 'balance' had eluded me at university, it was still way off my radar here. My friends and I would go out on a Friday night and continue boozing all through the weekend. At the time, I lived in an apartment in central London which became the base for everyone to meet up. We named it The USS Enterprise after the aircraft carrier in the film *Top Gun,* and each of us had a drinking nickname after a character in the film. Mine, fittingly, was 'Jester' because, let's be honest, I'm a bit of a clown. We'd meet there on a Friday evening after work, go across the road to a pub called The Hog in the Pound, get absolutely smashed, go back to mine, continue drinking, wake up on Saturday, do the whole thing again, go to sleep, wake up on Sunday and continue proceedings. So by the time Monday came around, not only was I a complete mess, but also not in the right frame of mind to be conducting any business.

In my first week at Diageo, I actually missed the first three days of work because I was coming off a massive bender from the weekend and too hungover to go in. In truth I was more than likely still drunk. Either way, I definitely wasn't being responsible.

Since this behaviour happened pretty much every weekend, I developed a system to cope with the Monday hangover. I would arrive at the office, go straight to the downstairs canteen and order the greasiest breakfast you can imagine. You could literally see your reflection in the grease. This 'cure' consisted of two sausages, a fried egg and a bagel with butter and Marmite. I had read somewhere that fried eggs and Marmite are good for hangovers and in the state I was in, I wasn't going to question the information. This was the only way to soak up the booze.

For pretty much that entire year, this was my life. Looking back, I can't help but laugh at how ridiculous it was and how ridiculous I was. Diageo has always promoted a culture of responsible drinking; this is something they drill into their employees. I was definitely not in line with this code of responsibility when I was there and my behaviour was far from responsible. The way I binge-drank on the weekends made me not just a liability to myself, but also to a company that was paying me to do a job. What I was doing was highly irresponsible and also disrespectful. Today I am someone who values the importance of hard work and dedication. I can clearly see that these were traits that I was void of back then. At the time, of course, I couldn't see this. I was unaware of how my drinking habits were causing me problems. Because I wasn't dependent on alcohol, and because I couldn't be classed as an alcoholic, at least in my understanding of what an alcoholic was, I really didn't see how it was getting in the way of my life.

ƒ

Since I've started my self-work, I've come to realise that I was drinking as an escape from the reality of having a job. Not because I hated my job. I actually really liked it. But I was living in the past and trying to 'escape' back to my university days.

As I mentioned in the chapter on divorce, I've always craved a sense of belonging. At university, I was part of the hockey team, who basically became my family for the three years I was there. Not only did we play hockey together, we also socialised together and a couple of us even lived together. Whenever we went out drinking, it was usually the same group. This made me feel I was a part of something and I loved the feeling. So much that I never wanted the nights to end and I never wanted to miss a drinking session. So when I left university and started working, I did whatever I could to keep my 'family' together. That meant a lot of drinking.

There are many who like to have a drink at the end of the week or the end of the day to unwind from work and that is more than acceptable. But when it's used as an escape from reality, the consequences can be problematic. And that goes for anything in life. I was firmly a 'weekend warrior' at this time—a person who would look to the weekends to escape. And while I would have told you then that I was living life to the fullest, looking back I most certainly wasn't. As I've mentioned, one of the biggest learnings since starting to work on myself has been the importance of living in the present and enjoying each and every day. What I have come to learn is that there is often guidance and learnings to be found in every situation in life, even if those learnings might not present themselves in a manner that is immediately apparent. Therefore, it's important to honour every moment. Maybe if I had lived more in the present instead of in constant anticipation of the weekend during my year at Diageo, I would have left with more learnings, not just about business but about life as well.

After Diageo, I moved to India and drinking as an escape only got worse. Sure, I had more than my fair share of great nights out. But a large number of them were an escape from reality. I hadn't wanted to be there. I was a fish out of water in India and I was certainly drinking like a fish. But at the time I convinced myself that it was fine because 'I'm young and carefree'. This justification was a bit of a theme and it took me years to finally recognise how everything I'm talking about in this chapter was having an adverse effect on me.

I remember this one Thursday night we went out for dinner to a Mexican restaurant. Even though I knew the next day was a workday, I got absolutely smashed without any regard for my professional commitments and then went back home and continued the party there. I was so hungover that I spent the next day in bed. I was a disaster.

The song *Grenade* by Bruno Mars was hot at the time and it had played through the night. That song still triggers me today, reminding me of that night and of the irresponsible way I used alcohol. That night, I had definitely been drinking to numb myself from the misery I felt from being in India.

The funny thing is that it took me eight years after

leaving India to see that I had been using alcohol as an escape and, therefore, the wrong way. Let's also bear in mind that I come from a family that produced the stuff and I had been working in the industry at the time. Yet, despite my close proximity to alcohol, I was totally unaware of my own drinking habits. This just goes to show how often we are totally unaware of our own behaviour. It requires tremendous amounts of self-discipline and self-awareness to see what we are doing. I can say that I have both of these things now, but I definitely didn't during my time in India! Hindsight's a wonderful thing, isn't it? It can be used either to make us feel super guilty or it can be used as a super teacher. If used as the latter, it can help us see our own past behavioural patterns, which weren't apparent to us in the moment, with much more clarity. And this can help us learn in order to continue moving forwards.

I will say this again: I would never have classed myself as an alcoholic when I was in India or at any point in my life up until then. I certainly was never dependent on it. In fact there were times when I went off the sauce for weeks and even months. But something someone once told me really stuck with me. That is, 'It's not how much you drink, it's how you drink.' And while I may not have been drinking enough to be classified as an alcoholic, the *way* I was drinking could definitely be classified as problematic.

ʃ

Six or seven years ago, something else started to happen when I drank. I got massive amounts of anxiety. This began in my year at Diageo, but it really became problematic after I left India. By that time I wasn't drinking as much as I had when I was in India. In fact, I was drinking pretty rarely by all measures. However, when I did drink, no matter if I had one drink or ten, I would wake up the next morning with crippling feelings of anxiety and paranoia. This would send me into a dark, downward spiral and have a major impact on my productivity and overall mental well-being for days afterwards. I used to get really worried about having done something or said something bad the previous night. When I was younger, I had definitely said things and done things to people when I was sauced up that I shouldn't have. So firstly, if you are one of those people, then I'm sorry. I hold my hands up and I apologise to you deeply. Now eight years later, I was scared of acting like that again. There was always a part of me that was like, 'Well, you've acted badly before, it's inevitably going to happen again.' And that really got me into an anxious space.

I would call my friends in a panic and ask if I had done something wrong. They'd say, 'No, dude, you were fine, chill out.' But this wouldn't bring me relief. I would have to call another friend to verify that what the first friend had said was true! It was a compulsive vicious circle.

What I didn't know at the time was that this fear was due to my OCD; that the obsessive way I called my friends up the next day was a compulsion to 'help' alleviate the pain caused by the obsessive thoughts. This form of compulsion is known as 'reassurance seeking' and the problem with it, as you can see, is that it is a never-ending spiral, as you constantly want reassurance over the reassurance. It's relentless and mentally draining.

At the time, I didn't know there could be a link between OCD and alcohol. I know that many people who drink have this sort of fear the next day. The term used to describe it is 'beer fear'. And if you suffer from that, you know just how guilt-ridden and anxious the days after a drinking session can be. Add OCD to it and you have a whole new level of paranoia!

One of the things I was most paranoid about was that I might have done something so bad that I would be sent to jail! To be honest, I find it hard to even write this with a straight face because of how absurd it sounds, but it's true! When I first spoke to my doctor about depression, I told him of this fear and he said it was known as a 'paranoid irrational thought'. Those of you who also suffer from paranoid irrational thoughts after drinking know that all logic goes out of the window and you believe those thoughts like they are the ultimate truth—no matter how outlandish or absurd the thought is.

My paranoia of jail might have stemmed from the fact that when I was nineteen, I was arrested for 'drunk and disorderly conduct in a public space'. I'm laughing while writing this and I don't know why. I'm not proud of it and I certainly don't condone this kind of behaviour. But I guess now that I've started, I might as well tell you about it. My girlfriend at the time and I had had a little bit of an argument after we left a London nightclub in the early hours of the morning, and being fuelled on alcohol, we had probably spoken a little bit louder than we should have. (I am loud on an everyday basis as it is. So add booze and you could probably hear me in Scotland!)

From what I remember, six police officers came running towards us out of nowhere. They questioned us and when I continued to speak loudly I was banged down and handcuffed.

I'm not going to lie: a part of me at the time thought this was really cool because I'd get a story out of it to share for the rest of my life. In that sense, I guess I wasn't wrong because here I am telling you about it fourteen years later! But let me continue the story.

After I was handcuffed, I was put in the back of the police van and taken off to the station. Because I was a very stubborn human being, I shot my mouth off the entire ride, asking the police officers to sing songs with me and take pictures. They were far from amused and, after checking me in at the station, they put me in a cell for the night. The next day a psychologist came by—apparently I needed to be evaluated before I could be released—and after this, I was let out. Thinking back, this was actually my first encounter with a mental health professional!

A couple of weeks later, I met my mom for lunch and she brought me a bag with my mail in it. One of the letters was from the transport police informing me of the fine I had to pay. Now my mom's name also starts with 'S' and she had read the name on the envelope as 'Mrs S. Mallya' instead of 'Mr S. Mallya' and opened it. So now not only did I have a fine to pay, I also had to explain to my mom why I had the fine in the first place!

This incident might have planted a seed in the back of my mind that one day I was going to do something so awful when I was drunk that I would end up in prison. As I mentioned earlier, perhaps going to court when I was nine during my parents' divorce also had something to do with this fear because, after all, courts and jail are in the same realm! And, looking back, it might have also stemmed from my fear of loneliness. I had always thought of jail as a very lonely place for one to be in: away from friends, family and those who bring you comfort and security. So the thought of being in that environment played on my fears of feeling alone and abandoned.

Then, of course, my dad's legal situation didn't

help. He was being accused of a number of different things and the headlines about the case against him included words like 'jail', 'arrest', 'bail', 'deportation'. All of that also just added fuel to the paranoid and irrational thoughts and fears about jail that I would have.

The time I would waste worrying about the night before, and the paranoia I would feel, eventually led me to the point where I thought, 'Clearly alcohol is not having a positive effect right now in my life, and I have some deep self-work to do.' And that's when I decided to stop.

I never said how long I'd stop for. I never put a timeline on it. I never said it would be forever. I said, 'Right now I need to focus on myself and get my mental well-being in order, and when, or if the time is right, I'll re-introduce it.' At the time of writing this chapter, it has been three years since my last drink and I have not regretted the decision one bit.

ʃ

How did I finally stop? This is a question I am asked over and over again by those looking to make a change in their lives. The answer is that I literally just decided to stop! It was as simple as that. I had a conversation with myself, weighed the pros and the cons of drinking, looked at whether it was an advantage or disadvantage in my life at that current moment, saw that I had much deeper psychological things going on that were being triggered by the alcohol and decided to stop till I sorted myself out. That conversation with myself led me to make the change.

I would say that if anyone is ever in a similar boat as I was, it's worth having a conversation with yourself. An honest conversation with yourself will help you see if something is having a positive or negative impact in your life. I now do this for pretty much anything. Asking yourself whether something is advantageous or disadvantageous to you will help you see what you need to in order to make a decision. And everyone is different. Some people might want to cut it out completely like I did, whereas others might just feel the need to cut back a little. The only one who knows what is best for you is you. I would say, try a few different approaches and see what works for you. You will only know what works and doesn't work for you by giving it a go. For example, there were times that I would go weeks, even months without booze, and I found that easy to do, no problem. The anxiety would stop, and I would feel at peace. But then when I started drinking again, even if it wasn't a lot, the anxious feelings, paranoia and obsessive thinking would start up again. I realised then that the only way I could work through my issues was to give it up completely.

✗

I've often been asked about peer pressure since I stopped drinking. A common theme seems to be the worry that one will no longer have or enjoy a social life, or will be ostracised by friends if one decides to stop or cut back on alcohol.

All of us have felt peer pressure. Whether it's the clothes we wear or the music we listen to, most of us have dealt with the feeling that we need to alter our behaviour in some way in order to fit in. But I've learnt the importance of just being happy with yourself, and that the only person you have responsibility for is yourself. So instead of looking at doing things to please others or gain approval or acceptance, we need to focus on what is most beneficial for us. By making ourselves and our happiness, health and mental well-being our priority, it becomes easier to say no to people, as it comes from a place of self-love and self-care.

That's the 'spiritual answer' to the question, but the straight 'no bullshit' answer would be this: If those friends of yours truly cared about you, they would support you no matter what you do, what you wear, what you listen to and whether or not you drink. I'm very fortunate to have an incredible group of friends who support me through everything. And they know that I'm there to support them unconditionally as well. If our friends can't support us, then they probably aren't as good as friends as we thought they were. I mean, if you decided to become a vegetarian, no one is going to force you to eat a piece of chicken, so why should someone force you to have a drink if you don't want to? A true friend might not agree with your decision, but will support you no matter what.

As I've said, my family business has been alcohol, particularly the manufacture of beer. Kingfisher, one of our brands, has a famous slogan: 'The King of Good Times'. What I say is, 'Be the king or the queen of your *own* good time.' If that means alcohol is not part of it at this point in your life, then so be it!

One of my biggest learnings with regard to alcohol is the importance of balance in life. Balance was something I more often than not did not have when I drank. And this lack of balance showed in other areas of my life as well. I believe that balance is central to well-being, both physical and mental, and it's something I'm definitely working to incorporate in all areas of my life today.

five
OCD and Me

Writing this chapter has been the most challenging of all, because to write about obsessive-compulsive disorder when you suffer from obsessive-compulsive disorder is very triggering!

I have suffered from OCD since my early childhood and have come to learn that it has been at the centre of many of the issues and much of the distress I've experienced in my life. I've tried to figure out when and how it started, but it has been hard to pinpoint. I was clinically diagnosed with it only at the age of twenty-nine, when the psychiatrist my GP had sent me to did a full evaluation of me. I remember reading his report and being like, 'I already knew I had OCD! Why the fuck have I paid money to come to you to tell me something that I already knew!' But since then I've realised that my understanding of OCD only scratched the surface.

Until I started working with my therapist, I had an idea of what I *thought* it was, but not what it *actually* is. I most certainly wouldn't have categorised it or even thought of it as a mental disorder. I know I'm not alone in saying this, because OCD is often one of the most misunderstood mental conditions there is and the term is terribly misused. How many times do you hear someone throwing around a statement like, 'Oh my God, I'm so OCD!' Most of the time the person saying that doesn't actually have a clue what OCD is. A reason for this lack of understanding is that OCD doesn't get the attention it deserves as a mental disorder. The severity of it and the distress it causes is rarely appreciated by those who don't suffer it.

I found the best description of the condition in a very good book my therapist gave me. *The Mindfulness Workbook for OCD* defines it as: '...A psychiatric and psychological mental health issue ... An *obsession* is an unwanted, intrusive thought. This type of thought may present itself as an idea, image, impulse, urge, memory, or other internal information, and you experience it as unwanted and distressing. A *compulsion* is a behaviour designed to reduce or avoid the discomfort that comes from your experience of an obsession. This behaviour may be physical, such as washing or checking, or mental, such as reviewing or neutralising ... *Disorder* describes something that's not contained or not as stable as it should be. It's out of order: *dis*ordered.'

Basically, if you're an OCD sufferer, you have an obsessive thought that can cause you great discomfort. You then feel compelled to carry out a compulsion in order to neutralise the pain. So far this might not sound all that troubling: you have a thought, do something about it. The difference though, between someone with OCD and someone without it, is not simply the thought, but the consequences you believe will follow if you don't engage in a compulsion. Everyone has distressing thoughts, but people without OCD are able to let the distressing thoughts go, whereas for those with OCD, the thought registers more on their mind's radar, making them feel like they *have* to do something about it.

You might be a little surprised to read this, because there seems to be a common belief that OCD is really just about being neat and tidy and about things being straight and in order. I probably was guilty of thinking this myself at first. Now, after researching the disorder, I've come to learn the full nature of the illness and how many different types of OCD there actually are. Yes, being neat and tidy is a part of OCD, but it's only one part and is known as 'Just Right OCD'. There are other forms of OCD, such as 'Responsibility Checking OCD', which could involve the compulsive checking of things over and over, such as whether you locked your door. 'Harm OCD', which deals with intrusive thoughts of a violent nature and the fears associated with that. And 'Scrupulosity OCD', which primarily focuses on a fear of God and religion. I have at one point or another dealt with issues that fall into each of these categories. At the time though, I was totally unaware that the behaviour I was engaging in was because of OCD.

Some people suffer just one aspect of OCD and not another. Or different things at different times. For me, 'Just Right OCD' was a big issue growing up. I suffered 'Harm OCD' after nights out drinking. And 'Scrupulosity OCD' (which I didn't even know was a word until I started doing work on it) has probably been the most distressing of all the OCDs I've dealt with.

The common understanding is that OCD can be treated, but it can never be cured. It is what is known as a chronic condition. It is very distressing and can cause sufferers immense amounts of pain and mental anguish. I don't think this information is widely understood or even widely known, so that's why, on behalf of all of the OCD sufferers out there, I wanted to take a little extra time at the beginning of this chapter to highlight what exactly OCD is before getting into my own experiences.

While working with my therapist has been vital for me on my journey with OCD, the amazing workbook I quoted from above helped me see all the different types and fully gain an understanding of the condition. It also gave me tools to deal with my OCD on a daily basis. I will reference this workbook throughout this chapter and at the end I'll discuss it in a little more detail. So now for my experience…

*

As a kid, I was very 'superstitious' and engaged in some very outlandish rituals and behaviours because a little voice in my head told me that if I didn't do these things, I would get bad luck. Indians are notoriously superstitious, and growing up, there were so many things I was told would bring bad luck if I did them that I was constantly on edge.

'Bad luck' for me was an umbrella term for anything bad, such as failing a test or losing a hockey match or being teased by my friends. Anything that could cause me pain or discomfort. It worried me so much that all anyone had to say to trigger me was that 'I would get bad luck' for something and my mind would go into overdrive to try and figure out what behaviour I had to engage in to make sure that didn't happen.

One Sunday at boarding school, we had the day off to go home. My best friend Ed and I decided to go to London for the day. Ed was a playful guy like me and he knew I was very 'superstitious', so he decided to fuck with me. He told me that if I stood on a crack on the street, something bad would happen. For the rest of the day, I literally tiptoed around the streets of London like I was some sort of fucking ballerina out of the Bolshoi ballet, trying to avoid stepping on cracks in order to avoid getting 'bad luck'. Now that the idea was in my head, this behaviour continued back at school. I walked around Wellington trying my hardest not to step on cracks. It got so bad that I would turn up late to class because a walk that should've taken me two minutes took ten.

It wasn't just what other people told me though. It was also what I'd tell myself. If my mind came up with a scenario where I could potentially get 'bad luck', I would come up with behaviour I thought I had to do to avoid it. Most of the time, though, there was absolutely no correlation between the behaviour and what I was trying to avoid getting bad luck for.

The fear of 'bad luck' plagued my whole time at boarding school. My compulsions not only got in the way of my own happiness and peace, but they also got in the way of my studies and they got in the way of the other kids' peace because my behaviour was a disturbance to them. To give you an example of this, in our boarding house, our bedrooms lined both sides of a corridor. One of my compulsions would be to open and shut my door over and over again before I went to sleep, otherwise I thought I would get 'bad luck' the next day. And the number of times

I would have to open and shut it would always have to be an even number. For example, it could never be twenty-five times, it would have to be twenty-four, or twenty-six (yes, it could be that many!). Except it couldn't be twenty-six because half of twenty-six is thirteen and that was an unlucky number. That's how my mind operated. Obviously, the sound of this opening and closing door was a disturbance and there'd be cries of 'Sid, just shut up and go to sleep' from the kids in the other bedrooms. It really irritated them and quite rightly so. But my mind wouldn't let me rest until I had done it a certain number of times.

Yet no matter how much distress the behaviour caused me, no matter how much it annoyed my friends, and no matter how much time I wasted in engaging with it, the fear of potential bad luck was far worse. This way of thinking pretty much ran my entire life.

It was only many years later that I came to learn that the reason I was having these thoughts and engaging in this kind of behaviour was because I was suffering from OCD. The thoughts about getting 'bad luck' were obsessions; the behaviours I came up with in response to the obsessions were compulsions. And because it was getting in the way of my well-being, it was a disorder.

Looking back, I wish I'd known that I was suffering from OCD because maybe I would have been able to get the help that I needed, not only to save me the anguish at the time, but also to save me from the mental distress that I would continue to suffer post school because of it. But back then, mental health wasn't something that was ever really spoken about, and OCD most certainly wasn't something I had even heard about.

ʃ

OCD continued to play havoc with my life after I left school. It got really bad when I was living in India and working for the Royal Challengers Bangalore cricket team in the Indian Premier League. Working in professional sport was a massive OCD minefield for me because I believed my actions during games could somehow directly impact the result.

I could only take a sip of my drink at certain points in the match. I could only blink when certain players were doing certain things. I could only speak to people during certain breaks. All of this was because there was a voice in my head saying, 'If you don't do this, Sid, you're going to bring your team bad luck.' In the 2010 season, at a time when we had lost a few games, my friend Aashish and I had a shot of tequila before an evening match (because when you're young and stupid, that's the sort of thing you do). The team won that night. So guess what? I started believing that to continue winning, Aashish and I had to have a shot of tequila before every game. If Aashish wasn't with me, I'd call him up and we'd have a shot together over the phone.

Now, I know people have rituals and superstitions when it comes to sports. A lucky jersey, a lucky mascot and so on. The rituals I had were straight-up OCD compulsions because if I didn't engage in them, I would believe the worst-case scenario would play out and that would cause me massive amounts of anxiety. Now there was, of course, always a part of me that knew my compulsive actions were not going to have any impact on the results of the game. After all, these were professional athletes playing a team sport with many different variables that could affect the outcome of the game. But the fear of what *could* go wrong if I didn't do the compulsions would always be stronger than the rational voice inside me, and the OCD would win every time.

Since I've started my self-work, I've learnt that this type of thinking is known as 'catastrophising', which basically means you believe that if you don't do a certain compulsion, things will go sideways and a worst-case scenario will play out. This also falls under a category of OCD known as 'hyper responsibility', which makes you believe you have a responsibility to stop certain things from happening and the way to do that is by engaging in compulsive behaviour—even if that compulsive behaviour is irrationally shooting a shot of tequila at ten in the morning! I know this story might sound amusing and looking back, it was. But I share it just to highlight how I was engaging in OCD tendencies without even knowing it.

So far all this compulsive behaviour that I used to engage in might sound funny or even eccentric. I can understand why. But trust me, if you have OCD, it is far from funny. To have these obsessive thoughts constantly screaming in your head is painful and brutal, and the compulsions you do to try and nullify the obsessions are equally painful and time-consuming. It gets to a point where you waste so much of your life energy engaging in this behaviour that it just sucks any happiness out of you. To the outside world, you come across as plain weird. On the inside, however, you believe it's an absolute must otherwise everything will fall apart. It might not sound like much, but it's crushing.

ƒ

Out of all the different types of OCD, there have been two particular types of OCD prevalent for me. The first is what is known as 'Harm OCD' and the second is known as 'Scrupulosity OCD'.

Harm OCD

Harm OCD is the fear that you might hurt someone, among other things. This is what I would experience after a night out on the sauce, when I'd wake up the next day with the morbid fear that I may have done something bad or hurt someone. And in order to deal with my obsessive, paranoid irrational thoughts, I would engage in compulsive behaviour. Two of the main compulsions I would engage in were 'reassurance seeking' and 'mental review'.

'Reassurance seeking' meant I would call my friends up to ask if I had done anything bad during the night. If they said no, I would call another friend to verify what the first friend had said. Even if the second friend reiterated what the first had said, I wouldn't be satisfied. I would sometimes go as far as to Google crime and police reports from the area I had been in the night before just to ensure I hadn't done something bad and forgotten about it. That's the level of fear I had. But despite getting the answers I wanted, the obsessive thoughts would continue. This would drive me to seek more reassurance from other sources. And this would go on for days. Like I mentioned in the previous chapter, what I came to learn about reassurance seeking as a compulsion is that you are never satisfied; you seek reassurance for the reassurance. This causes you to end up in a never-ending vicious circle until the OCD mind finds something more exciting to latch on to.

The second compulsion was 'mental review'. Mental review is basically playing out a scenario from the past in your mind over and over, hoping to remember it exactly. For me this involved playing out the night I had been drinking over and over in my mind, hoping it would help me see I hadn't done anything wrong. The issue with this, though, is that we don't remember everything we do at the best of times, so add alcohol into the mix and memories and moments are distorted or spotty at best. Again, this compulsion would go on for days and, like reassurance seeking, mental review doesn't work because you're never satisfied with the answer you get. That's partly because when you think about the past, you think about it and experience it from the present moment. So whatever you come up with is not actually the past or what happened, it's a distorted view of the past based on what we are currently experiencing and feeling at this present moment in time. This means that when I tried to review the previous night, it would be with the anxiety I was experiencing in the present moment. This anxiety, coupled with not being able to remember everything exactly, would just add to the fear that I had done something wrong.

Harm OCD was one of the main reasons I stopped drinking. The anxiety, paranoia and fear, coupled with the time I would waste the next day with my compulsive behaviour, outweighed the enjoyment of drinking from the night before. Now, however, should I ever choose to start drinking again, it will be with the ability and clarity to see where these thoughts and fears come from. I will know they are a part of OCD and not based on truth, so I will be able to deal with them in a rational and objective manner without getting lost in them.

Scrupulosity OCD

The best definition I've found of scrupulosity is in *The Mindfulness Workbook for OCD*. There is an entire chapter dedicated to this type of OCD because it seems to be quite prevalent amongst sufferers. It says: 'Scrupulosity OCD targets people who place a high value on philosophy, religion, life rules, or laws, and existential meaning. It's often referred to as *religious* OCD but it can follow the same trajectory for non-religious moral concepts. People with religious scrupulosity focus primarily on the idea that they are failing to adhere to the rules or intents of their subscribed religion.'

Simply put, scrupulosity OCD is a fear of religion and a fear of God. For me it was the constant fear that if I wasn't perfect, or if I didn't do things the perfect way, I was going to be punished by God. An obsessive fear of God drove me to compulsive behaviour to avoid perceived punishment or 'bad luck'. It has caused me immense amounts of psychological suffering over the years and, in terms of OCD, might have been the thing to bring me the most pain.

I didn't always fear God. When I was younger, I was actually very religious.

At boarding school, I kept religious artefacts on my bedside table and, every night before going to sleep, I would say a Hindu mantra along with my own prayers. I'd thank God for the day, my family and my friends. It was a loving experience. At school, I had to attend chapel pretty much every morning. I loved it. I loved the Lord's Prayer and Grace and I loved singing the hymns. (Still, to this day, I know every word of *Jerusalem* and *Dear Lord and Father of Mankind*!)

Back then, I believed that all gods were different. There were Christian gods I'd pray to in chapel and there were Hindu gods I'd pray to when I was on my own or when I visited temples with my family. Either way, though, I'd say I had a good relationship with prayer and with God.

I don't know what caused what I'm about to share next, but during my time at Wellington, something came into my head that, because I was not a Christian, I shouldn't be singing the Christian hymns or saying the Christian prayers. I somehow started feeling that if I did, I would be angering the Hindu gods because, after all, I was a Hindu. Angering the gods would result in them punishing me or giving me bad luck.

At this time, my night-time prayer also started becoming compulsive. Instead of being a calm, loving experience, it became a stressful compulsion to avoid bad luck. I started praying to God, asking him to please help ensure that none of the bad things I was afraid of happening would happen. The problem, though, was that these 'bad luck things' would often still occur. And when they did, I would just assume that it was because I had done something wrong and I was being punished by God. My belief was that if I was being good, then surely God would have answered my prayer and ensured that the thing would not have happened.

Obviously, I now see that there was really no correlation between the 'bad luck' and my prayers. The 'bad luck things' were just things that happened as part of life, so they were going to happen regardless of how many times I prayed. Back then I couldn't see this, though, so my relationship with religion, which was initially based on love, fun and freedom, very quickly turned into one based entirely on fear.

This fear of God then started to rule pretty much every part of my life and only got worse as the years went by. Now, however, the fear was no longer 'bad luck', it was being 'punished by God'. Punishment meant literally anything that could cause discomfort. As we know in life, numerous things cause us discomfort on a daily basis. But instead of viewing these as natural occurrences, I viewed these discomforts as punishments from above.

When I got to India in 2010, my fears and

compulsions were taken to another level. At home I believed I had to go to the prayer room and pray every day. If I didn't, I would be punished. But this wasn't all. I believed I had to be a hundred per cent 'clean' to enter the prayer room, so I would literally wash my hands and feet twenty times. If on the way to the prayer room, my hand touched something, or if my sleeve brushed against something, I would have to wash my hands again and change my shirt. If I touched the fresh piece of clothing with that same 'dirty' hand, that piece of clothing would now also be dirty and I would have to find a new piece to wear.

Things were just as bad once I finally went into the puja room. I was scared of touching anything. I was scared of doing anything because I believed that if I didn't behave 'perfectly' I would anger God and be punished. The prayer room experience caused me massive stress.

Then my prayers themselves became problematic. I believed that if I didn't say thank you for everything that had happened that day, I would anger God and I would be punished for not being grateful. I believed that if I didn't say my prayers with grammatical perfection, I would be disrespecting God and I would be punished. I believed that if I didn't 'feel' the gratitude enough during my prayers, I wasn't grateful enough and would be punished. This would drive me to say my prayers again and again to ensure that I'd said every word perfectly. I would go through the entire day again to ensure I said thank you for absolutely everything that had happened. I would say things over and over again just to make sure I was feeling enough gratitude. Because of this, a prayer that should have taken me a few minutes would end up taking me an hour.

Now I'm getting tired just writing about this, and I'm sure you might be finding it a little tiring to keep up with everything I'm talking about! Well, just imagine how mentally and physically draining it was to actually engage in the behaviour!

What I was doing wasn't worship. It wasn't giving thanks. It wasn't giving love. It was compulsive behaviour stemming from fear. It was straight-up Scrupulosity OCD. And it made me want to hate God and hate religion. For so many years I had felt I was treading on eggshells. I had felt as though there was a man in the sky ready to punish me for not living life perfectly.

Much of the problem lies in the words 'perfectly' and 'properly'. As we know, perfection doesn't exist. Perfectionism is also a type of OCD and the problem with it is that the closer you get to achieving 'perfection', the bar just gets raised. So I could never live a life that was up to the standards that 'God' had set for me. What I see now is that it wasn't God at all. It was my OCD.

I can't pinpoint exactly how or when my

scrupulosity OCD started, but working with my therapist, I have an idea: My grandmother is a very religious person. Throughout my life, she has promoted the idea of an angry god who punishes. If something doesn't go our way, she will say it's a 'punishment from God'. This is her core belief, and something I've heard her constantly go on about. I remember her saying to me on this one occasion when I was younger, 'God will be very angry' in response to something I was saying. This stuck with me and I feel it might well have been one of the building blocks of the image I came to have of a vengeful, angry god. After all, a child is inclined to believe what a parent or grandparent tells them, so it makes sense that I would take what she was saying as gospel (no pun intended). On this point, it's fascinating to see how so much of our fears and even the way we view ourselves later in life stem from comments made to us by adults when we are children. This is definitely something we should all keep in mind when talking to the young!

Many of you reading this might find what I'm talking about straight-up weird, but those who might have experienced something similar know just how tormenting the experience can be. A fear of God can cause massive distress simply because there is no running from it. You are taught growing up that 'God is everywhere', so really there is no place you can hide. Looking back, it makes me sad to see how much I struggled with this idea of an angry God because divinity should be something we can turn to for comfort, guidance and support.

But I'm happy to say that in the last couple of years, I've started to get over this religious scrupulosity. Learning that there is such a thing as scrupulosity OCD and that it is a legitimate part of the illness helped me realise that my fears of God were based on obsession and not on any spiritual teachings or truths. This took a tonne of pressure off me. While these fear-based thoughts still pop into my head, they no longer run my life.

A couple of years ago, my view of religion changed. I don't know how it happened, but I had something of a divine awakening. I started seeing God as an essence that is within all of us. I went from what I would say was religious to spiritual and now I am back to being rooted in unconditional love, guidance and support.

ʃ

I have mentioned *The Mindfulness Workbook for OCD* through this chapter and I'm going to mention it again now. Even though it might seem like it, it is NOT AN ENDORSEMENT! No one is paying me to talk about it. The reason I mention it throughout is simply because it really was life-changing and I want to ensure that as many OCD sufferers know about it as possible. The book, written by Jon Hershfield and Tom Corboy, got me to really understand what I've been dealing with. If you want to fix something in life you need to understand what the problem is first. This book not only shone a light on OCD as a whole, but also on the specific aspects I suffer from. Now when something comes up I can easily identify it and say, 'Oh that's my perfectionism' or 'Oh, that's my scrupulosity OCD', and I can see it, I can accept it and I can let it pass without the automatic reaction of a compulsion.

When you suffer from OCD, you really feel as though you're out of control and you have to do things in order to stop other things from happening. This workbook taught me that, at the end of the day, we have choices and doing compulsions is a choice. When you get comfortable with understanding that you don't have to do your compulsions in order to live, and you get to a point where you can let the obsessive fear pass, life becomes a much more pleasant experience.

Since I worked through it, I feel more freedom, more at ease and calmer than I have at any other time in my life. To be honest, doing the workbook hurt. It hurt a lot. That's what happens when you first shine a light on any mental illness. So if you are going to take the plunge and get this book or something similar, don't expect the process to be easy. It is going to hurt, it is going to be painful, it is going to be brutal. But I promise you, it is worth it. No amount of pain is worse than the pain that OCD causes, so if you are willing to fight through the unease to do the work in the book, I can tell you the results will be life-changing. I'm living proof of that.

ʃ

Believe it or not, I have actually seen some benefits come out of my OCD. This might sound like a fucking strange thing to say given everything I've said so far, but it's true. The one thing that living with OCD has taught me in the long run is acceptance. As painful as our thoughts might seem at times, they aren't us, and they can't actually hurt us. I know this is something that many struggle with (OCD sufferers and non-OCD sufferers) because we tend to believe we are personally responsible for our thoughts. Then what we end up doing is fighting the thoughts because we don't believe they belong in our heads. OCD has taught me that trying to fight your thoughts is like trying to fight the weather outside. It's a fight you can't win. They're going to happen whether you like it or not, so your job is not to try and remove them or change them, but to simply mindfully accept and allow them.

The other benefit I've found from having OCD is that it is great for acting! Now bear with me as I try and explain why. We are always taught as actors to have a strong thought process during a scene, because strong thoughts lead to strong behaviour. OCD thoughts cause strong emotional responses within (and they are going to occur whether I like it or not!), so I was like 'Well, why not embrace them and incorporate them into the scene!' By doing that, I've found a way to accept them and actually use them to my advantage. As they say, there is always light to be found even in the darkest of times, so incorporating the disorder into my craft has actually made it easier to deal with!

Have these obsessive thoughts stopped? No. And they never will. But at least now I see where they come from, and more important, I can see that they are not me but part of a mental condition. OCD is chronic so it's always going to be there, but once you learn how to manage it, it becomes a lot easier and doesn't end up running your life.

six

Built on Guilt

Feelings of guilt have been something I have dealt with throughout my life. And despite all my self-work, guilt is probably the most prominent of all the things I still deal with today.

While working with my therapist, I discovered that these feelings of guilt seem to stem from my upbringing in a family that had wealth. Many people through the course of my life made comments and passed judgements about my family background and our perceived wealth as though it was somehow bad and it was my fault that I was a part of this family— something I had no control over. I was made to feel like an outsider, and at times somewhat of a villain. This led me to feel and act in certain ways over the years and developed into something of a complex.

If I'm honest, writing this book has at times triggered those feelings of guilt. That's because a little part of me feels as though I'm perhaps a fraud for talking about the issues I've gone through because I come from a stable background (financially at least; emotionally, not so much). People may, therefore, think I'm just 'complaining' and being ungrateful. This is a fear that I have come to learn stems from the judgement I received growing up and for the way it was assumed that I had it 'easy'. But mental ill-health can affect any of us, regardless of upbringing, background and financial status, and I've had to remind myself of this at times while writing.

Before we continue, I think it's important for me to say that I do acknowledge that I had a very fortunate upbringing, from a material point of view at least. While the family I was born into has at times come with a lot of weight and baggage, I would be lying if I said that it didn't also open many doors and give me some great opportunities along the way. For that I am and will always be grateful. Therefore, this chapter isn't me complaining about my background; it's me merely sharing how certain judgements aimed at me because of it ended up having a lasting mental effect.

✗

So, as I've mentioned, I was made to feel guilty for my background from a young age. Kids at school would make comments like, 'Oh, you're so rich, your family's this, your family's that...' Most of the time this was said with an undertone of sarcasm or scorn. The irony, though, was that my school was a private prep school in the Royal County of Berkshire, meaning that the parents of those kids who were passing judgement weren't exactly badly off themselves.

Even the teachers would chime in and mock me on occasion. Once, when a new student who came from Middle Eastern royalty joined our class, our form teacher said, 'Boys, we have a new student who might make Sid look poor.' What a fucking stupid thing to say to a class of eleven-year-olds. Now I get that the teacher was trying to be funny, but comments like that, as well as the ones being made by my classmates, made me feel like an outsider. I became embarrassed by my family, so much so that when my father was in town and wanted to drive me to school, I would beg him not to do it because I didn't want the other kids to see his car, even though the car wasn't anything out of the ordinary compared to what the other parents were driving. I just wanted to avoid any chance of being judged.

While at school, I was also made to feel different at times because of the colour of my skin. I, like so many young kids in the UK who have coloured skin, suffered racist abuse during my childhood, and I was teased relentlessly for it. But if I'm honest, it was the comments about my family that would affect me more than the ones about my ethnicity.

I also remember that I had a nanny once who point blank told me to my face that I was spoiled. I remember that comment like it was made yesterday. I had just been picked up from school and was sitting in the back of the car. I must have been seven years old.

The truth is, she was probably right. Compared to most children that age, I was probably given a lot more, so I might well have been classed as spoiled. Nonetheless, I don't think that is a comment you make to a child. (As I said in the previous chapter, I think people say things to young children without much thought. Maybe because they think they are so young that it won't affect them or that they will soon forget about it. But the fact that I can still recall that day and write about it twenty-six years later shows how incorrect that thinking is.)

As I have since discovered, comments like this made me feel subconsciously that I had an unfair advantage over others. And they would be the building blocks for the guilt I would come to feel.

One statement that I've had thrown at me constantly is that I was 'born with a silver spoon in my mouth'. Wherever I've gone, whatever I've done, people have said this to me. Once, at Mumbai airport, the immigration officer took my passport, read my name and said, 'Ah, the boy who was born with a silver spoon.' I wanted to punch him. It is one of the dumbest comments that can ever be made.

It seemed that everybody had an opinion about me based on my family and I was being judged for something I had no control over. These sorts of remarks also reiterated the belief I had in the back of my mind that I somehow had an unfair advantage over others. I felt undeserving and super guilty and it drove me to want to hide my last name.

Often then, when I'd meet new people, they'd introduce themselves with their first name and last name. But when it was my turn, I'd just say, 'Hi, I'm Sid' and stop there. I found it very difficult to say my last name. I was scared that if anyone heard it (particularly in India), I would automatically be judged for it or treated in a different way, which would make me feel guilty. What these sorts of comments also did was instil a belief in me that I was nothing more than my last name; that I was only a worthwhile person because of the family I came from.

♪

So that's where the guilt stems from, and as you will see, guilt has continued to show up in different ways throughout my life and led me to do certain things. What I have come to learn is that all this guilt can in some way or another be linked back to my family background, and the judgements that came from that. The things I'm going to talk about next are in no particular order; they are just some of the areas where I feel the guilt has shown up the most.

Feeling guilty for feeling!

When I first encountered depression, I continuously told myself to snap out of it. I would run through a monologue, saying, 'Come on, Sidhartha, snap out of it. There are those in the world less well off than you. You are so fortunate. You shouldn't feel this way.' Trying to talk myself out of how I felt not only made me feel worse, it made me feel super guilty as well.

Since doing my mental health work, I've learnt that this guilt stemmed from feeling as though I somehow didn't have the right to be unhappy because everything from a material point of view was fine in my life. Somehow, I felt as though I was being ungrateful for the life I had. I have realised that this mindset can be traced back to my early days, when people made comments about my family's wealth. It made me develop a belief over the years that, because I had a fortunate upbringing, I could not feel the way I had felt during the depression.

When I was first starting acting, I was dealing with my complex about my family background and how I might be judged for it. My acting coach, Anthony, said, 'Pain is pain. Your pain is no less and no greater than the next person's pain regardless of your upbringing or your background.'

This was very eye-opening. I realised I had been judging the 'ease' of my life based on what others said about me, as opposed to fully appreciating what I had actually been through. As such, I had been stopping myself from feeling and experiencing emotion because I saw it as 'ungrateful' or 'fraudulent' behaviour.

For example, the experience of my parents' divorce was painful and had a long-lasting effect on me. But I guess because of comments I heard, I never really appreciated the pain I felt. I almost grew to believe I wasn't allowed to feel pain because, materially, things had been okay for me. Now I see that my thinking was totally skewed and the pain I felt was just as much and just as valid as the pain experienced by someone who might have come from less. This took me a long time to embrace, but it has helped me feel less guilty about my upbringing.

Giving to avoid feeling guilty

I live my life by a simple saying, which is that if you can make one person smile a day, then you've done your bit to make the world a better place. One of the things I like to do is give food to those in need. I think it's a simple gesture that can go a long way in helping someone. But if I'm honest, there are times I do it out of guilt. For example, if something really good happens, or if I've just made some money, a part of me will feel guilty for it. I will feel that I already have so much privilege that it's unfair to be given more. This will compulsively drive me to help those less fortunate than me in order to 'balance' things out.

Now don't get me wrong; I want to give what I can to those in need, as I feel that we have a social responsibility to help others where we can. But I think what you can see here is that sometimes that action stems from the fear of feeling guilty. When the root of any action is fear, it becomes problematic. Because if you don't act, you'll beat yourself up and make yourself feel even guiltier, which just adds fuel to the fire.

The need to 'prove' myself

When I moved to India, I started to get a lot of attention in the media. As much as I loved it, I knew I was only getting it because of my family name. After all, I hadn't done anything at that point on my own yet to be recognised. This not only made me feel like a bit of a fraud, but guilty as well. A lot of this stemmed from the fact that many of the articles would refer to me as 'Vijay Mallya's son'. Seeing myself being referred to as someone's son sort of solidified the feeling I had going on within that I didn't deserve the attention—something that continued even after I started to work. This, coupled with the numerous people who would constantly comment on how 'easy' my life was and jump to conclusions and judgements without knowing anything about me, made me desperate to prove that I was more than just my surname; that I could be my own person. This was definitely a part of my initial decision to pursue a career outside the family business.

When I finally decided to leave India, there were many who even made me feel guilty for the decision I had made. Friends and family members made me feel I was some sort of Judas and terrible person for 'turning my back' on my dad. One friend told me how, if it were him, he would never have left his father. Another said that if her brother had decided to do what I did, their dad would have slapped him! I'm really not sure what they were trying to achieve by telling me this, because my decision to pursue another career path had absolutely no bearing on their lives! But it did make me feel guilty. To this day, my grandmother will tell me how my dad sold the business because I didn't want to be a part of it. I've had others tell me that this simply isn't true (I mean, let's not forget that he does also have two daughters, so it can't have been all because of me!), but hearing something like that will obviously make anyone feel an element of guilt. It took me a long time to finally get over these feelings and move on in peace. The interesting thing, though, is that the only person who has never made me feel guilty about my decision to leave the family business has been my dad. Since his opinion in this situation is the only one that matters, it's best to let the other barking dogs bark.

The need to prove myself got in my way at the beginning of my acting career. Whenever I got an audition, I'd put an immense amount of pressure on myself because I always saw the audition as the thing that, if I got the part, would finally allow me to be able to say fuck you to all those who judged me and made me feel I was no more than my family name. Because of this, there was a sense of desperation around what I was doing because the motivation to get the role stemmed from a place of fear as opposed to a place of security. When fear is your motivation, things don't tend to work out. As I learnt!

I'll never forget the excitement when I got into drama school. British drama schools are incredibly tough to get into. There is an intense audition process and the acceptance rate is really low. My particular course only had twenty spots on it and thousands of applicants. When I woke up to find an email saying I'd been offered a place, I felt content and happy with myself because I felt like I'd achieved something on my own. I knew I'd got in because of the work I did, and that my family had nothing to do with it. This made me feel worthwhile. What I have come to realise, though, is that what I was seeking was external validation, and getting accepted gave me just that. The issue with this, though, is that if we are reliant on others or things to make us feel worthwhile and complete, we are on dangerous ground. All that needs to happen is for that thing not to work out and we will be back to feeling either inadequate or guilty.

We can get so caught up in trying to prove things to others that we lose sight of what it is we are actually trying to achieve. It took me a number of years after getting to Los Angeles to finally accept that the only person you have to prove anything to is yourself, and since I have, it has taken the mental pressure off much of what I do and made the whole process much more enjoyable. I also learnt that there are people who will continue to say things even after you have achieved something yourself. The comments go from 'How lucky you are!' to 'Oh, you only got that because of your privilege and family'. There will always be those ready to try and take things away from you and bring you down, no matter how much you do in life. Therefore, today everything I do is for me because I know people are going to have opinions and make judgements regardless!

Doing, doing, doing

Because of the way I was made to feel about my background, I developed this belief that I always have to be 'doing' something to 'justify' the privilege and the opportunities I've been given. This led me to believe that I always have to be working and 'doing', which made it very hard for me to switch off. If I ever did, the voice in my head would tell me I was being lazy and wasting the opportunities. And that would make me feel guilty.

When it comes to the arts, I pick things up at a very quick pace. Three years ago, when I was taking singing classes, the teacher said to me that I had the ability to take her notes and incorporate them very quickly. While this was great for my learning, it made me also feel very uncomfortable because I have developed a belief over the years that if something comes easily to me, I don't deserve it. And if I get it, I feel guilty for it. So I end up going out of my way to make whatever I'm doing harder for myself, just so I can 'feel' I worked hard and, therefore, deserve it.

This showed up a lot in my acting work, especially when working on a scene. In drama school, we were taught a very specific method of breaking down a scene, what to look for, how to make choices, etc. After a while, though, once you do it enough, things start coming naturally and instinctively. It's kind of like learning to drive a car. When you first learn, you have to consciously think about all the things you're doing: check the mirrors, hands on the steering wheel, adjust the seat, etc. But after a while all those sorts of things become second nature and you don't have to think about them.

But I couldn't let go of that whole process I

had been taught. Not because I was being diligent or thorough with my work, but because if I didn't go through the whole process I would feel I was 'cheating', and 'cutting corners' or worse, being lazy. So I would end up doing this whole process, and more than I needed to, just to tick a mental box in my head simply to feel like I was working hard, to avoid feeling guilty. It was compulsive behaviour. This is something I did pretty much in all areas, not just in regard to acting.

Something strange I discovered was that it would take five days after I achieved something for that voice in my head to say, 'Do more'. I called it the five-day rule. For five days after I, say, achieved a breakthrough in my self-work or in my acting or in the gym, my mind would let me have that achievement. It would let me feel happy and content. But on the fifth day, the voice in my head would come back, saying, 'Right, that's enough. What's next?' And this would make me feel I had to do more. If I didn't, I would feel guilty.

This compulsive 'doing' was not benefitting me or my work. Constantly being on the go, constantly feeling I had to be doing something and not taking the time to switch off was actually having a detrimental effect on my mental well-being and what I was trying to accomplish. The constant 'doing' also destroyed any sort of work-life balance I may have had. It drained me of energy, it stressed me out, it made me anxious. And the overall quality of the work I was doing suffered because I was doing too much without taking the necessary time to look after myself in between.

I did an entire episode in my ConSIDer This series on the importance of switching off. A lot of people cringe at the idea of taking a little time to themselves. They somehow feel they don't deserve to, and if they do they're just being lazy or even selfish. But while it is important to work hard, it is just as important to take time off for your physical and mental well-being. Since I've started doing this, my stress levels have reduced and the quality of what I do when I'm working has increased, as has my efficiency. This was very uncomfortable to not just admit at first, but to incorporate as well. It definitely triggered my guilt. But the more I stuck with it, the more comfortable it got.

Writing this book gave me an opportunity to practice taking time for myself without feeling guilty for doing it. When you take a deep dive into your past and open up about issues you've suffered with, it can take quite a mental toll on you. I didn't really think about this when I set out to write the book. At the beginning, I would say, 'Today I'm going to write X words', and then maybe a quarter of the way into it, I'd feel mentally and emotionally drained. My initial reaction was to keep powering through to avoid guilt for not hitting my goals for the day. I soon realised, however, that that would be compulsive doing and it wouldn't be beneficial for my well-being or for the book. After all, there was no point writing a book about mental health if I didn't take care of my mental health in the process! So I learnt to stop and take my time.

Perfectionism

Perfectionism is another aspect of the guilt I feel that stems from the belief that I have had an unfair advantage in life because of my background. I often thought that in order to show gratitude for what I had been given, I needed to be perfect and do things perfectly.

If I wasn't doing things perfectly, I would think God would punish me. Or I'd get bad karma from the universe because I wasn't doing justice to the opportunities I had been given.

Obviously, I couldn't reach the standards I set because, first, perfection doesn't actually exist, and second, it is unobtainable. If I ever got close to being 'perfect', the standards would just get higher, so I constantly felt I was failing, which made me feel guilty and distressed. It was a vicious circle.

What I have learnt is that perfectionism is a form of OCD, and these fear-based thoughts I had about wasting opportunities were just obsessions. Since recognising this, I am able to far better separate the times when I actually do need to be doing more work, from the times when I'm just feeling that way because I'm looking to avoid feeling guilty.

Guilt due to the divorce

Issues of guilt have also been prevalent in my relationship with my mom. After the divorce, my mom and I moved house and it was then just the two of us living together.

Of course, my life with my dad and all the privilege that came with being his son continued. I continued to go on amazing holidays with him. I continued to be given elaborate gifts. For my mom, however, it all stopped. Financially she was stable, but everything else that came from being a part of our family came to an abrupt end. And through my life, I felt really guilty for this. That I was able to continue reaping the benefits of being a part of my dad's family, whereas my mom lost all the opportunities that had once also been hers. Even to this day I feel somewhat uneasy whenever I tell my mom about what I do when I'm with my dad because a part of me doesn't want to make her feel bad or left out in any way.

A couple of years ago, we were chatting in the kitchen soon after the new year. I don't remember how the conversation got on to this, but I said something to her along the lines of how happy I was when I was with her. What she said afterwards was really quite emotional for me. She said she had always worried that she couldn't give me an exciting life when I was growing up, like my dad could, so she was happy to hear me saying this. When I was with him, I got to travel the world and live a very fast-paced and entertaining life. And then I would come home and go on about how much I wanted to live with my dad and his other family. Of course, as I've earlier mentioned, this was just emotion and misdirected anger talking at the time, but I never realised how it would affect my mom. Hearing her say this brought up all my feelings of guilt and I explained to her that what I had had with her growing up had been a very real life and something I was grateful for.

ſ

My issues with guilt have been hard to shake and continue to cause me a great amount of mental torment. I'm glad to say, though, that the more work I do on it, the better it gets. I'm learning to fully embrace and accept who I am and where I came from. I'm growing to accept that I can't change it and I'm certainly not going to lie about it. It's my truth, and as uncomfortable as it is talking about it, at the end of the day, it's my reality and I'm learning to own it without fear of judgement. This has helped me feel much less pressure in what I do and made the journey of life far more enjoyable.

seven

Sad about Dad

Throughout this book I've talked about my dad's 'situation', so it's probably time to actually explain to you what the situation is in slightly more detail.

My dad is a very prominent Indian businessman who has a larger-than-life personality. He works hard and plays hard as well. His main business was alcohol, particularly beer. The main brand, Kingfisher, is one of the most recognisable brands in India today. After taking over the company at the age of twenty-seven, following his father's sudden death, he grew it into a leading global conglomerate with business interests in different areas, such as sports, hospitality and pharmaceuticals, amongst others.

One of the businesses he launched was an airline called Kingfisher Airlines back in 2005. Kingfisher revolutionised the aviation industry in India. It connected cities that had never been connected before and it really changed the meaning of luxury travel in the country. People loved the product. But due to business issues, such as the financial collapse of 2008, amongst others, the airline ran into trouble. This was where the problems started.

I'm not going to get into the specifics of what happened because this isn't a book on that. But to cut a long story short, my old man started being accused of a number of different things by the Indian government, such as fraud, deception, money laundering, collusion and other things that would make you think he is some sort of criminal mastermind. The news channels covered this extensively and he was painted as a villain.

In March 2016, he left India for the UK where he had been a resident for over thirty years. The news channels then accused him of having 'fled the country', 'absconded', and 'run away'.

Since then, he has been fighting a hard legal battle with the Indian government, who is trying to have him extradited back to India to face several charges. This has seen him get arrested in the UK and released on bail and attend court on numerous occasions. It has caused him huge amounts of stress on a daily basis and it has caused me much anguish to witness. Just writing about it reminds me of what a surreal experience the whole situation has been. To put it into perspective, about twenty years ago, my dad was involved in a helicopter crash. I remember how distressing that was to hear about at the time. Well, for me, that incident pales in comparison to this current saga! I should mention at this point that my old man maintains he is innocent of these charges and that he hasn't done anything wrong or illegal.

The whole ordeal has been a very public affair. Newspapers and news channels have been covering it and, in the world of social media, everyone has had their say. There has been nowhere to get a break from it. I am reminded of the situation on a daily basis, which has been mentally exhausting and draining. Since I live in the US, I am somewhat distanced from the coverage, but anytime I go online, there is always a reminder of what is happening. There is the stress of wondering what could actually happen to my dad from a legal point of view and also the torment of knowing he is suffering and I can't do anything about it.

I don't think I fully appreciated the effect my dad's trouble was having on me at first. It probably took a couple of years to fully sink in and for me to allow myself to feel and acknowledge just how distressful it was.

This chapter is not about me commenting on the legal aspect of the case and I am certainly not attempting to sway your opinion about my dad.

What I am going to share with you is how the ordeal has impacted me on a mental and emotional level.

The pain of watching a loved one suffer

Watching someone you care about as they suffer definitely has an impact on you, especially if you're an empath like I am. Though my dad and I might not have had the closest of relationships in recent years, it still hurts to see him deal with the stress he endures on a daily basis. Knowing there is very little I can do to actually help adds to the pain and also causes immense amounts of frustration.

When I was in the UK, I attended a couple of his court sessions with him. The process of going to court in the first place is a surreal experience. Going there because of a case against a parent really fucks with your head. It was difficult to see him sit in the dock behind some glass. It looked like he was confined in a cell more suited to Hannibal Lecter. When the judge asked him to stand up as she read some stuff out, I felt pain and helplessness. It was like I was at the zoo, watching an animal in a cage.

Growing up, one of my favourite films was *Liar Liar* with Jim Carrey. The courtroom scene near the end of the film when Jim Carrey's character wins the case is one of my all-time favourites. Because the script was so good and because Jim Carrey is such a genius comic actor, the film would make you think that the experience of being in court was quite a fun thing. However, what I saw first-hand from being in court with my dad that day was far from fun or entertaining.

Upon leaving these court hearings, we would be greeted by the media outside the courthouse, all aiming questions at my dad. Most of them were not questions, however, but accusations and statements. Basically anything that would cause him to react and thus generate the best news. Hearing some of the things aimed at him was very difficult to deal with, and seeing his frustration build was hard to watch. I prayed that he would keep his cool and wouldn't say anything in the heat of the moment. After all, these reporters were trying to poke the bear in the hope that he would react. Fortunately, my dad remained calm for the majority of the time.

There is one picture of the two of us coming out of the court after one of these hearings, and in my suit, wearing sunglasses, I almost look like my old man's bodyguard. As sharp as I looked on the outside, I felt nothing like that on the inside, and those sunglasses were there to hide the pain and tears in my eyes that were coming off the back of what I'd just seen.

Not long ago, I was on FaceTime with my dad, and I felt as though he had lost his spark. I could see that what he was going through was taking a big toll on him. If you ask him, though, he might have a different view. He always likes to say how tough he is. And the truth is, he probably is a lot tougher than most people. One of his lawyers once said to me that not many would have the resilience my dad has shown over the past five years to keep fighting. But while this might be true, he's certainly not bulletproof or immune to the toll a situation like this can take on one's mental health. On that FaceTime call, I could see that, despite the strength on the surface, there was anguish and pain behind his eyes. As they say, the eyes are the window to the soul and they don't lie. This hurt to see.

My dad is also a very emotionally guarded individual, so as much as I want to be there for him, I always feel as though there is a wall between us. This frustrates me, as I wish he would just open up.

A couple of years ago, when we had a big chat I mentioned earlier, when we agreed that we were just very different people at this point in our lives, he told me he realised that I was a 'super sensitive individual'. (Had he said that five or six years before that conversation, I would have taken it as a big insult because, like vulnerability, I would've seen sensitivity as weakness. Now, however, I felt it might have been the greatest compliment I'd ever been paid in my life! That's because by then I had come to realise that being super sensitive and vulnerable can be our biggest strengths as human beings. And my dad noticing this in me was the result of my self-work!) On the flip side, I told him that I see him as a 'super guarded individual' and this is where the difference between us lies. I think his generation has a very different view on what being 'tough' means. For his generation, toughness is shutting off, compartmentalising, putting up a wall and not showing your feelings. For me and those of my generation, real strength comes from letting your guard down and allowing yourself to be vulnerable.

This was a great reminder, though, that everyone is different, and people have different views based on a number of different factors—age, upbringing, etc. For those of us who have gone through a process of self-work, we might wish people were more open with us or behaved in a certain way, but we have to remember that everyone deals with things in their own way. Those who grew up in a different time, and those who might not have worked on themselves may see and deal with things differently, and that is okay. For example, if the Sidhartha of today tried to have a chat with the Sidhartha of ten years ago about being vulnerable and open, the younger version would have probably punched the present-day version in the face. That's simply because the junior me hadn't done the work on himself and, therefore, wouldn't have been able to relate or even comprehend what the present-day version of me was saying. Therefore, it's important to have compassion.

Maybe after reading this book, my dad may

finally allow himself to be vulnerable and open, but maybe not. Either way, I need to learn to become comfortable with who he is and the way he chooses to express (or not express) himself. After all, if you have gone through the kind of mentally, emotionally and physically stressful ordeal that my dad has, isn't it only natural to try and protect yourself as much as possible? If that means he puts up a guard, I must accept it and learn to work with it.

In fact, since learning to work with it, I have actually seen a shift in him. Yes, the guard is still there, but a softer side of him has emerged. They say that you get reflected back at you what you put out, so by acknowledging and accepting him as he is, there is less resistance from me, and in turn less from him being reflected back.

The other person it's been really difficult to see over this time has been my grandmother. My grandmother has always been full of life; the sort of person you will find doing shots of tequila with my friends. (This actually has happened, btw!) She is very independent and sharp. But as my father's mother, she has also suffered tremendously having to see what her son is going through. She loves to watch the news (especially Indian news), so she's constantly seeing and hearing things being said about her son. My grandmother also tends to succumb to negative thinking, and if she sees something written or said about her son, she first of all always believes it and second, always goes to the worst-case scenario. What's funny is that she lives with my dad, so she actually has first-hand access to the man herself to find things out, but she still likes to believe what she sees and reads!

In the last five years, I have been a sort of agony aunt to my grandmother; the person she can complain to and share her fears with. We literally couldn't have a conversation without talking about my dad's case and her worries. As much as I wanted to be there for her, it got to a point where it actually got too much to take and I had to tell her to stop calling me up if she wanted to talk about my dad's situation. This was simply because I was trying to deal with my own feelings on the situation, so having to take someone else's load as well was just too much to handle. I will say, though, that being able to tell her to stop was actually one of the biggest steps on my journey of growth. Like many people I have always put others first, but while I think this is a great quality to have, I have come to learn that if it comes at a cost to your own happiness or mental well-being, it really isn't a very responsible way to live.

I'm sure you think this sounds selfish, and to be honest, I worried too at first that I was being self-centred. But as much as we all want to be there for others, we have to ensure that we look after ourselves first, or we aren't going to be much use to anyone else. The best analogy for this is the safety instructions for oxygen masks on a plane. In the demonstration, the instruction is to 'first put your own mask on before helping anyone else'. That is sort of what I had to do when it came to talking to my grandmother.

Watching my dad and grandmother suffer over the past five years has been very emotionally challenging. Watching anyone suffer isn't a pleasant experience, but when it's two people so close to you, there is an extra dimension of pain.

The pain of public persecution

Everyone has family drama. But for most people, that drama is kept within the four walls of their home and dealt with in a private manner. Our drama has been public. It has been all over the newspapers, the news channels, social media, you name it. When you see news channels, other media outlets and also members of the public use words like 'thief', 'fugitive', 'loot', 'arrest', 'jail' in relation to a parent, it can be very traumatic to see and take. The way this case has been covered in the press makes me feel a mix of anger, disappointment and frustration. Anger for the way my old man has been portrayed as a master criminal. Disappointment at some of the blatantly untrue things that have been reported. And frustration at the way members of the public believe everything they are told and abuse us for what they believe to be fact.

What I have learnt through this ordeal is that when something is public, everyone and their mother seems to feel they have the *right* to comment and pass judgement even if they don't have all the facts. I'm a big believer in the right to an opinion, but I also feel we have a duty and responsibility to know all the facts before we form that opinion. Sadly, though, we live in a world where people can get their opinion across with the click of a button, so the process of diligence required to form an opinion in the first place is usually missed.

Most of the messages and comments haven't been opinions, though. They have been vindictive attacks and outright abuse. If I were to even begin to share some of the messages I have received on social media over the past few years, I'm not sure this book would be allowed to be published! Let me just say that some of the things that were said have been outright hurtful, nasty and, quite frankly, savage. No one should say or write such things as 'I hope you and your family die', regardless of whether they have the right to an opinion or not. There is a difference between an opinion and trolling. Sadly, many people tend to forget the difference.

I did a ConSIDer This episode on online abuse and trolling. People have asked me how I deal with it and I wish I could say that it doesn't affect me, but the truth is it does hurt. When I was younger, I learnt the rhyme 'Sticks and stones may break my bones, but words will never hurt me'. In my wise old age I've learnt that this rhyme is complete bullshit. Of course words hurt. In fact, a lot of the time words can hurt more than physical pain. When you have messages like 'I hope you die' and 'I hope your family goes to jail', it really hurts. Anyone who tells you otherwise is either made of stone or flat out lying.

Because we live in a digital age where everyone's life is online in one form or another, it's almost as if people no longer think before they type. Because they don't have to interact with anyone face to face, they believe they can say whatever they want, free of consequences. What people forget, though, is that while there may not be consequences for them, there are still consequences for the person who is being abused. Because when you leave a comment on a picture, it might seem like it's just words you're typing in response to a photograph, but there is a real human being behind the photo who has real human feelings. Therefore, when people comment they aren't just commenting on a picture they are directly affecting a real person. Sometimes, I see a message and I think perhaps they've forgotten this because I wonder if they would actually come and say the same sorts of things to my face.

One of the most painful terms that has been used by members of the public to describe my dad has been 'traitor'. There is a belief that because he left India, my dad 'fled' the country with the money he supposedly took. Again, this is because of the narrative that has been spun around him. But if there is one thing I can say with absolute certainty about my dad, it's that he is not a traitor. You can use pretty much every word in the book to describe him, but traitor isn't one of them. Everything the man has done over the years has been to put his country on the map. Whether it was naming his Formula One team Force India or bringing artefacts of national significance back to the country, he did it all out of pride and a love for India. So hearing him referred to as a 'traitor' is especially hard to take. You would be hard-pressed to find a more patriotic person.

But how can I blame people for the opinions and judgements they form? We are a society that sadly is conditioned to believe what we are told. Most of the time we don't do our own research. When the media says that this man is a 'thief' and a 'crook' and that he actually stole YOUR money (part of the narrative was that my father stole money from public banks which is taxpayer money), what are you meant to think? Coming to this realisation helped me a lot because I started viewing these 'abusers' with compassion instead of anger. Does it still hurt to get abusive messages? Of course. Does it still frustrate me to have inaccuracies aimed at us? Of course. But at least now I have a way to look at it objectively.

Also, not all the messages have been of hate.

Many have been loving and supportive. People I have never met before and who I probably never will meet have reached out from all over the globe. They remind me to focus my attention on those who brighten your light as opposed to those who try and extinguish it.

The pain of people's rejection

The most difficult part of this ordeal has been seeing those who have been close allies and friends for so many years turn their backs on us. I've always been an overly trusting person, and the betrayal we endured from certain people has felt like a dagger in the back. The line '*Et tu*, Brute?' from William Shakespeare's play *Julius Caesar* comes to mind. Anyone who has ever been let down by anyone (and I would sadly imagine that is the majority of those reading this) knows the pain it causes.

My dad's generosity has always matched his larger-than-life personality. Maybe it's the only child in him that loves to be surrounded by people, but you probably won't find many as generous to his friends as my old man. Now, those who were always the first to show up when times were golden have run a country mile from him when the times haven't been so good. I've always valued loyalty as one of the most important qualities in a person, and to see the way people can turn on you has been eye-opening. Or maybe I have simply just been a naïve human being up until this point in my life. I don't know. What I do know is that seeing this happen has been truly heart-breaking, and a mindfuck to say the least.

They always say your real friends will emerge when times are tough and certainly this situation has helped me see who those real friends are. Many have been a constant support through it all and to them I will forever be grateful. But the ones you thought you could count on but haven't been there stand out. A part of you questions how close that person actually was to you in the first place, and this is disappointing on so many levels. There have been times through this all that even though deep down I've known people have been there for me, I have felt alone.

ʃ

A few months ago, I watched the Netflix documentary my dad was featured in. Watching it, I felt a mix of emotions. Seeing the way he was being portrayed made me feel angry, it made me feel sad, it made me feel guilty, it made me feel heartbreak and it made me feel disappointment. I think the best way to describe it is a rollercoaster of emotions. The type that goes at four hundred mph and does twenty-five upside-down twists and turns; the type you come off feeling nauseated. This is probably the best way to describe everything I've felt over the past five or so years.

But this situation has taught me resilience. As Winston Churchill said, 'If you are going through hell, keep going', and that is certainly what I've done throughout the whole ordeal. Despite the mental anguish it has caused me, I don't believe I've ever let the situation defeat me. Also, for the past three years or so, I've done it without alcohol or anything else to 'numb the pain'. So I can safely tell you that no matter what life throws at me, I have the resilience and strength to be a rock for myself. Often we don't know what we are capable of until we have experienced something challenging. This situation has been that 'something' for me.

Everything I've spoken about in this chapter has been ongoing at the time of writing this book (April 2021), and it seems there will still be a long way to go. Legal proceedings can take their own sweet time, so I'm not sure when we will see some sort of resolution. All I know is that however long it takes, I will continue to do my very best to show up for myself in whatever way I need to in order to keep marching forward and to keep looking after my mental health and well-being.

eight
(What Helped Me) Be Free

Everything I've spoken about in this book so far—the discoveries, realisations and learnings I have had—has only been possible because of the deep amount of self-work I've done over the past three or four years.

So, to end with, I want to share with you some of the things I've found to be especially helpful along my self-work journey. What I say might not work for everyone and this is certainly not a self-help book. These are just things that have helped me, so I thought it would be worth putting down for you.

✦

We all strive to be the best sons, the best daughters, the best partners, the best fathers, the best mothers, the best siblings, the best friends, and what I have learnt is that in order to do that, we have to get our own houses in order first. Many people try and do this and then get told that by focusing on themselves they are being selfish. In reality, working on yourself is the most selfless thing you can do. Self-work doesn't mean you have to give up your life and go on some 'eat, pray, love' trip. There are many ways to work on yourself and look after your mental well-being wherever you are. All you have to do is figure out what works for you, and be willing to commit.

The best way I have found to define self-work is by splitting it into the two words *self* and *work*. For the word *self*, it's important to remember that you are doing the work for yourself and no one else. So taking things at your own pace and doing things that work for YOU should be the priority. The only person you have a responsibility to is yourself, and the only person who knows what works and doesn't work for you is you. So it's important to keep yourself as the focus throughout the journey.

As for the word *work*, it's important to remember that if you want to see results in anything in life, you have to put in the effort. So remember that you will only get as much out of it as you are willing to put in. There will be times when the work is uncomfortable, there will be times when the work seems overwhelming, and there will be times when you question why you are doing it at all. But as I found, if you stick with it, the results and the quality of life you can achieve are unparalleled. I sometimes prefer to refer to it as 'practice' as opposed to 'work' because it can help to take a little pressure off.

All right, that's my little spiel. Let's get into it.

Therapist

As you probably have gauged through this book, working with a therapist has been the single most important thing for me. Everything I've discovered and the person I am today has stemmed off the back of the work I've done with my therapist over the past three-and-a-half years. Dr Danika Zivot is one of the most wonderful people I have ever met and she has literally transformed my life. I couldn't write a book as open and as vulnerable as this one without her. She has opened me up in ways I had never felt before and, through encouraging me to revisit my past, has helped me identify the root causes of a lot of pain that I carried around for years.

Not only does she make me feel guided, she also makes me feel supported and safe. In fact, in some acting exercises, when we have been asked to think about a safe and happy environment, her office has come to mind.

You will only get as much out of therapy as you are willing to put in, and someone who makes you feel supported and safe is more likely to make you want to open up. This was certainly my experience. The first therapist I saw when I was back in London didn't make me feel any of these things. I think it's safe to say I would not have got the same benefit or growth with the therapist in London that I've seen with my current therapist because I don't believe I would have let my guard down. So the help she would have been able to give me would have been limited, as she would only be able to give as much as I did.

Therefore, the most important thing when it comes to therapy is finding the right person for you. If that means trying a couple to see who you click with, go ahead and explore. When I asked my doctor in Los Angeles to refer me to therapists he knew, he asked if I preferred a man or a woman. This might seem like a small thing, but it actually has more significance than you might think. Throughout my life, it has always been the female teachers who brought out the best in me. Why that is I don't know, but I've definitely felt more comfortable and more at ease with the female presences is in my life. So I felt that working with a female therapist could help bring out the best in me. I use this as an example of the sort of things you might want to ask yourself when deciding on a therapist. For instance, if there are certain traits that you gravitate towards, be aware of them so you can find the right fit.

At the most basic level, just having someone to

talk to has been life-changing. When I first started, I would go in with a whole list of things I wanted to talk about. Just being able to get the stuff out in the open (bear in mind that it included some stuff I had never spoken of before) was very liberating. Because of my OCD, I would often go in with the same things over and over again each week, engaging in the OCD reassurance-seeking compulsion. However, no matter how many times I came back with the same thing, Danika patiently listened and walked me through what I needed. She never made me feel stupid and she never made me feel I was wasting her time. I would love to assume that all good therapists are like this because she never put any pressure on me and as a result I feel I was able to grow at a pace that was right for me.

I also learnt to measure growth over a period of time as opposed to week by week. Initially, I wanted to see results immediately, so would constantly look to see the growth after each of our weekly sessions. I would look to see if my thought patterns had changed, if I was feeling calmer, etc. Some weeks I would see a difference, and others I wouldn't. And in the ones I didn't, I'd get frustrated and beat myself up over it. But I learnt that I was expecting too much too soon. After all, what we were doing was reconditioning a lifetime of behaviour! Once I learnt to take my time and measure growth over months or even years instead of weeks, I was able to finally appreciate just how much I'd achieved and how far I'd come. So my advice here is to take things slowly! Just on this point, I also learnt to redefine what growth was. Initially I thought it was about removing all of the 'negative' experiences of life. Feeling sad, getting angry, getting stressed, etc. But what I came to learn is that self-work isn't about removing any of life's 'problems' but learning how to best deal with them. No matter how much work we do, we are always going to find ourselves in situations that make us feel angry, sad, irritated. That is part of life. Once I started to accept this, it took a great deal of pressure off what I was doing.

The other main benefit of therapy has been taking a deep dive into my past. If you want a flower to bloom, you need to get rid of the weeds underneath. So I had always wanted to revisit the past to see what had affected me and what I was holding on to, so I could finally work through it and release it. Having Danika to guide me through that has been amazing. Any dive into the past can be scary and uncomfortable, but I'm happy I did it because today I'm able to move on with my life without much of the emotional baggage I had from before weighing me down.

If you are willing to take that journey, commit to it a hundred per cent. It will be painful, it will leave you battered and bruised from time to time, but your freedom will be worth all the pain along the way.

Therapy has been life-changing for me and I think everybody should give it a shot if they can. I understand this isn't an option for everyone, but if you have access to it, I strongly suggest exploring it. There is still a slight stigma around mental health and therapy, but do remember that there is absolutely no shame or weakness in seeking professional help. In fact, admitting you need to speak to a professional and going through with it is one of the most vulnerable and, therefore, brave things you can do.

Meditation

I have been practising meditation for about four years now. In my mid-twenties, I probably couldn't have thought of an activity that sounded more boring, but now I can't imagine my life without it. Since I've started practising meditation regularly, I've become more grounded and much calmer overall. It's helped me get into a much better mental place to deal with the sorts of issues that life throws at us on a daily basis. It has also helped me with my issues of loneliness, as it has trained me to find peace within myself and to just sit with that peace on my own.

There are so many types of meditation that choosing one is like picking out a gym class. The only way to figure out what works for you is to try a few different ones out and see which one you enjoy the most. That is what I did and I currently practice transcendental meditation or TM, and Qi Gong.

TM is a form of mantra meditation which, amongst other things, has helped me with my restlessness. Sitting still for more than five minutes was always a challenge for me and TM trained me to just sit still and do nothing for twenty minutes twice a day. This has made me a more grounded and settled individual. If you are a restless person, this one might be good for you.

TM also doesn't seem to have any rules, which takes a great deal of pressure off because you feel you can't do it wrong. Many of us, when we start meditation, constantly worry whether we are 'doing it properly'. Sometimes we get so caught up in breathing right, sitting right, focusing right, that it can stress us out more than it calms us down! As with most things in life, if it feels like a chore, then chances are you won't continue doing it. That certainly happened for me. It was only when I found TM that I became totally comfortable with meditation.

Qi Gong is a moving meditation that I learnt back in drama school. I usually do it when I have a little less time, or if I just want a change from TM. The movements of Qi Gong are very grounding and help me feel connected to both my body and the earth below.

Running/Walking

I have found running to be a huge release. I was running long before I did any self-work, but that was just a means of getting in shape. Now, it's another form of meditation for me. Particularly if it's outdoors, as I find it clears my mind, helps me settle into my body and connects all my senses with nature and my surroundings. This, together with the endorphins that exercise naturally releases, always leaves me feeling good and relaxed afterwards.

I remember, back when I trained for the marathon in Mumbai, I ran around the racecourse at night. Being outdoors in the dark was so calming. It was like the busyness of the world was still going on around me, but I was in my own little space, disconnected from the hustle and bustle and stress of everyday life. For the hour or two I was on my run, I felt a sense of peace that I didn't feel anywhere else. I would come back feeling refreshed, re-energised and calm.

Even if you're not a runner, just going for a walk outdoors and reconnecting with nature can have a profound impact on your mental well-being. Not long ago I took a walk with my dog and found myself in awe of the natural beauty I was surrounded by. Whether it was the colour of the leaves on the trees, the shape of the clouds in the sky, or even just the touch of the breeze against my face, I found myself totally mesmerised by it all.

And it made me realise that we have a never-ending movie of beauty constantly playing right in front of us. Many of us turn to the TV or some form of electronic entertainment to keep ourselves occupied and forget that the world is doing this for us right in front of our eyes. All we have to do is stay present and be willing to see it! So just by going for a walk and allowing yourself to absorb all the sights, sounds and smells that are always in front of us, you can calm down and stay focused and present.

I like to call these walks 'wandering in wonder'. I allow myself to roam around in a relaxed state, taking in the natural beauty and miracles of life. Children have so much wonder and curiosity about everything they see. Everything is an amusement for them and life is one massive game. For some reason or another, we lose that playfulness as we grow up. But why should we? I've found that by incorporating that childlike wonder and playfulness into everything I do, I stay present and appreciate everything around me.

To remain present and engaged in my surroundings, I sometimes also play a couple of games. The first is the 'senses game', which is as simple as fully immersing yourself in your senses and describing what you see, taste, touch, smell and hear. The more detail you go into, the more engaged it keeps you in the moment.

The other is the 'alphabet game', where all you have to do is name one thing you can see in your immediate surroundings that starts with every letter of the alphabet. This is a fun one because some letters are really easy but others are extremely difficult and require you to really focus on what's around you.

Getting to know myself

You could argue that the whole process of self-work and self-discovery is about getting to know oneself. While I think this is true, there has been one very specific thing I have done which has helped me along the way.

When I started acting and was first learning how to develop a character, my acting coach asked me to fill out a thirty-question form about the character. The questions ranged from my character's name to his upbringing, his wants, dreams, desires and fears. Basically all the things that make someone human. Anthony said that to create a real, truthful character, we should know all these things. I've used this process ever since and it helps me add depth and truthfulness to my roles.

Then one day I was like, 'Hang on. If this process helps me find out so much about a character, maybe it can help me discover a lot about myself!' So I proceeded to apply the questionnaire to me. By being open and honest with the answers, I was able to see things about myself that I might not have necessarily been aware of before. Again, this is one of those things that you will only get as much out of as you are willing to put in, so if you do it, commit to doing it thoroughly. Remember this is for you and no one else ever needs to see it. It's for you to get to know yourself, so be as honest as possible. You might find out things that you may not necessarily like about yourself or there might be fears that you haven't admitted to before. That's all okay. By admitting to these things and shining a light on them, you can choose how to deal with them moving forward.

I have narrowed the list down to the twenty questions that I think are the most beneficial. (The original list of questions for character development included other questions that were more acting-specific.) Enjoy!

1. What do I love/hate?
2. What do I tolerate/never tolerate?
3. What do I find funny? What makes me laugh?
4. What makes me nervous?
5. What makes me angry?
6. What makes me scared?
7. What makes me happy?
8. What are my hobbies?
9. What type of personality am I attracted to?
10. What are my good habits?
11. What are my bad habits?
12. What are my dreams and desires?
13. What are my needs and obsessions?

14. What are my hopes? Doubts?
15. How (exactly) do I feel about myself? (Past and present)
16. What motivates me?
17. What did I want to be as a child and why? (Think of what you wanted to be at the age of five, the age of ten and the age of fifteen.)
18. How different am I compared to my dreams/goals/fantasies?
19. What, if any, are my regrets? (My actions? An event in my life?)
20. Do I have any addictions/vices? (If so, what and for how long? How serious is it? Have you ever needed/wanted help? Be very specific with this one.)

(This list was developed by Anthony Gilardi at the Anthony Gilardi Acting Studio in Los Angeles. Anthony was my first acting coach, and still remains close to me today. The studio has been my home away from home since I moved to Los Angeles.)

The power of listening

A lot of people reached out after my first-ever ConSIDer This episode on depression to ask what I think is the best advice a person could give to a friend or a family member who is suffering from a mental health issue. What I have found during my mental health journey is that often the best thing someone who isn't a mental health professional can do is to not say or do anything at all, but simply listen to that person when they come to you. In my experience, having a friend I could talk to and who truly listened without trying to 'fix' the problem was invaluable. It helped me feel less alone.

So if you really want to help someone, just work on becoming a better listener. If someone comes to you with their issues in the first place, it shows they trust you. This trust deserves to be respected. The best way to do this is to keep your mouth shut, your ears open and your focus completely on the other person. I can't even begin to tell you how incredibly disheartening it can be when you try to open up to someone and you can clearly see that their mind is elsewhere. One thing that really helped me become a better listener is doing what Eckhart Tolle says in *The Power of Now*: I 'listen with my whole body.' This might sound strange, but if you can imagine yourself listening with your whole body, it automatically takes you out of your mind and makes you more present and engaged with the person who is talking.

Dealing with people's opinions

Just about everyone today seems to have an opinion about everything we do. If we aren't careful, these opinions can have a negative impact on our self-esteem and general mental well-being. Many of us have to deal with being constantly told what we 'should' be doing, how we 'should' look, how we 'should' lose weight, when we 'should' get married, etc., and then we get worked up over this constant barrage of seemingly never-ending comments. There have certainly been times when I've wished people would just shut up and keep their opinions to themselves.

But I have come to accept in my not-so-wise old age that this is never going to happen. People are always going to pass opinions and judgements about us, so trying to stop them is a waste of energy. Over the course of my self-work journey I've learnt that most of the time the opinion itself isn't the problem. It is the value and importance we give the opinion, usually based on who said it, that can be problematic. So the game isn't about trying to stop opinions. It's about learning whose opinion to listen to and what to do with it instead. For that, I will share a few things that I have discovered to be very helpful.

First, it's important to remember that, even though they might seem like it, opinions aren't truths and they aren't facts. They are simply someone's view. So learning to view them as such and learning not to take them as gospel can help you decide which opinions to give attention to and which ones to simply let go of.

Second, trying to figure out whose opinions are actually worth taking into consideration and whose are not has been really helpful. For example, I constantly have people going on at me about how I'm too thin, and that I don't eat, and that I need to put on more muscle, etc. It's relentless. Now if it's just some punter telling me how bad I look just for the sake of it, it's not worth my time to mentally engage. But if my nutritionist tells me, 'Sid, you are too thin and it's unhealthy,' it's probably in my best interest to listen to him.

Third, don't be afraid to ask *why*. If someone gives you an opinion, they should be able to explain to you why and how they came to the conclusion they have. You don't need to be confrontational about it, simply ask. If they can't give an explanation, it's probably a remark that doesn't deserve much of your attention.

Finally, at the risk of sounding like something you find on the wall of a yoga studio, remember that YOUR opinion also matters. Therefore, you should do what makes YOU happy! I think we end up giving so much thought to what others think that we tend to forget to take our own views into consideration.

Dealing with online abuse and trolls

Internet trolling has become rampant. The minute we put ourselves out there, we automatically put ourselves at risk. I want to share a few things that have helped me deal with online abuse.

The first thing is to learn to simply let the messages go. Now I know this seems obvious, but it took me a long time to embrace. For the longest time, I'd get really riled up by abusive comments and my ego would go straight into retaliation mode. Then I finally grew up and realised that by retaliating, all I was doing was dropping myself down to their level, aggravating things and wasting precious energy that would be better focused elsewhere. So instead of reacting, what I did was accept and acknowledge that the comment was mean and didn't feel good, and then I simply turned my attention to more important things.

The second thing I did was use self-deprecating humour. I've always incorporated self-deprecation into my acting because I think being able to laugh at yourself is a great quality. And being able to laugh at yourself seems to totally disarm trolls. For example, someone once sent me a comment along the lines of, 'Sid Mallya looks like a dog' and I said something like, 'That's an insult to dogs.' The person saw they weren't going to get a reaction out of me and apologised. Most of the time, trolls are just looking for a reaction. So if you can show them that they aren't going to get one and they can't get under your skin, they quickly lose interest.

Finally, I just learnt not to take things personally.

I learnt that when people make nasty comments, all they are doing is holding a mirror up to themselves and projecting their own anger and insecurities onto us. So instead of getting angry, I started feeling compassion for them. Today, if someone writes something abusive, I will respond with either a red heart or a message of love because I know that, more often than not, the reason they are abusing me is because they are just projecting their own pain onto me. Since I've started doing this, a lot of people actually write back and say sorry for saying what they did. This is an important point that can be applied to anything in life. If you deal with a situation with hate or anger, you're more than likely just going to throw more fuel on the fire. But if you deal with it with love and compassion, you can more often than not put the fire out.

Playing with a pet

I don't think I really appreciated my dog, Duke, or the impact an animal can have on one's life until I went through my mental issues. The unconditional love a dog can give you is like nothing on the planet. So if you're ever feeling low, find an animal to play with. It really is therapeutic, and you get an abundance of love. Duke has also taught me patience and makes me want to be a better person.

Being flexible with yourself

Probably the most important thing I've learnt on my mental health and self-work journey is to be flexible. What might work for you today might not have much value for you tomorrow, and what might seem alien today could end up being something you resonate with down the line.

At our graduation ceremony at drama school, the actor Martin Freeman was given an honorary fellowship. In his speech, he said there were things he had learnt at drama school which at the time he had thought was the be all and end all of acting, but upon leaving never used once in his career. He also said that he had learnt other things which at the time seemed like total shit, but then twenty years later he found himself using that technique on stage. Now, of course, he was speaking in relation to acting, but I feel this can also be applied to working on one's self and life in general. We should be flexible and open to everything without dismissing anything.

Also around the time my class graduated from drama school, the actor Riz Ahmed came and spoke to us. He said that 'actors should be like jazz players'. So much of jazz is improvised. The musicians have to be totally open to anything; they have to be present and really listen to everyone in order to create the music. By likening actors to jazz players, I believe Riz was saying that we should be free, flexible and present. I found this so profound that I started using it as the basis for how I live my life in general. 'Living life like a jazz player' has made me a lot more open to seeing and accepting what's right in front of me, it's made me a lot more present and it has helped me get rid of judgements about the way things 'should' look or 'should' be.

On this last point, what I found on my journey is that so many times in life, we can have a preconceived notion about something. And if that something doesn't show up or present itself within our predetermined framework, we can end up missing it. I have learnt the importance of not having any judgements about anything. There is a Christian parable I heard when I was younger that stuck with me, which I use to remind myself of this. In the story (and I'm paraphrasing), a flood comes, so a man climbs onto the roof of his house to avoid going under. When he is up there, he prays to God to be saved. A minute later, a group of people row past in a boat. 'Jump in,' they shout. 'No,' replies the man. 'God is going to save me.' A few minutes later, a helicopter flies overhead, and sends down a ladder to the man. 'Climb up,' says the helicopter pilot. Again the man replies, 'No thanks. God will save me.' Finally, a person comes by in a motor boat. 'Come on, get in,' he says. 'Thanks for the offer, but I'm fine. God will save me.' Eventually, the water levels rise so high that the man ends up drowning. Upon arriving in heaven, the man is distraught and confused. He sees God and says, 'I have been a good person my whole life. I prayed to you to save me but you didn't come, and here I am, dead.' 'What are you talking about,' God says. 'I sent you a rowboat, a helicopter *and* a motorboat.' Now I don't want to turn into a religious preacher, but the point of this parable is to let go of expectations of the way we think things 'should' be. Instead, we should be open to everything that is presented to us and be flexible with our views because if we don't, we can miss the messages and guidance that's always right in front of our eyes.

Throughout this book, I've talked about how each of the issues I've dealt with have actually helped me grow in some way or another. Well, had I not kept an open mind about them, I certainly wouldn't have been able to see the sides of them that have been a positive.

ʃ

I'll end this chapter by saying what I started with: Only you know what works for you. What works for someone else doesn't have to work for you and that is okay.

When I started my own self-work journey, I was keen to read and learn as much as I could from as many different places as I could. I would finish reading one book, and then try and apply everything

I had learnt from it into my life. Then I would move on to the next book and try and apply everything from that book as well. (My desire to help myself almost became obsessive which, let me say, ISN'T helpful!)

Even if I didn't fully resonate with what the author had written, I would still try and force myself to apply it. If I couldn't, I would beat myself up and feel like I was failing to grow. It made the work I was doing stressful as opposed to liberating. Then one fine day I came to the realisation that all these books were written by people based on their own experiences in the world and where they were at that current moment in their lives. Therefore, while the overall messages and principles they talked about could be applied to my life, trying to follow everything down to a T wasn't something I could do, nor had to do. This wasn't because I was 'failing' to understand what they were talking about, but simply because I was a different person, living a very different life, with different circumstances to theirs. What I realised I was doing was trying to use these books as 'rules' to live life by, but what would be far more beneficial would be to use them as 'tools' to live MY life by. So, instead, I started taking the best bits I resonated with from each book, and modified them to fit into things that worked for me. Flexibility was the key here, and once I realised this, things started to really click for me.

Therefore, I would advise anyone who is on a journey of self-work to take everything they learn, read, hear, discover (even things from this book!), etc. and be flexible with it. Play with it. Modify it. Make it fit into your life. After all, this is your journey, no one else's, so make it work for YOU.

So to Conclude...

There we are. That's my story. I had initially thought that I would write some grand, 'intellectual' ending, but if I'm honest I don't really know what to say, so I'll keep it brief.

When I got the offer to do this book, I was over the moon. I was so excited to be able to continue sharing my experiences with the world in order to continue shining a light on mental health. But I'm not going to lie, when the writing started, I was hit with the reality of what it actually meant to write a book like this. The entire endeavour has at times been exhilarating but also exhausting. There have been moments where I've really enjoyed it, and others where I've completely hated it! It's made me laugh, it's made me cry, it's made me smile and it's made me scream. But knowing that there is a possibility that this book might help just one other person going through something has made the entire journey worth it.

As I said at the beginning, I hope that by being as open, honest and raw as I could be about my experiences, this book has been able not only to amuse where it can, but also to educate about various issues and how they can manifest. I also hope it might inspire others to go on their own journey of self-work.

For me, whilst I recognise I've come a very long way, I've learnt that the process of self-work is never-ending and the opportunities to learn new things about ourselves and grow are endless. Therefore, my journey is ongoing, and will be till the end of my time on this planet.

So let me end by once again saying thank you for letting me share my story with you. I know how much I put into writing this, so it means more than I can put into words that you have taken the time to read it.

Much love,
Sidhartha x

'Now this is not the end. It is not even the beginning of the end. But it is, perhaps, the end of the beginning.' –Winston Churchill

Acknowledgements

I have been blessed to have had so many people in my life who have helped, inspired, taught and guided me that this list of acknowledgments could be never-ending! Therefore, I will limit it to those who had a particular influence on me during my journey of self-work and self-discovery.

It's only right to start with my therapist, Dr Danika Zivot. Danika has been my guiding light through my whole journey of self-work. The care, support and guidance she has given me has helped me grow in ways I would never have imagined when I first started working on myself. I don't think there are enough words to express the gratitude I have for her.

I'd also like to thank:

Paul Kampf, for the consistent support and encouragement he gives me. I originally met Paul as an acting coach, but through the years he has become not just a coach, but also a friend and mentor, and is like family to me. Thank you for always believing in me and helping me to believe in myself.

Peggy and Bobby Rometo, for opening me up to a world of spirituality and connection to the divine far greater than what I could have ever comprehended.

The Royal Central School of Speech and Drama and all my teachers there for helping me to open up and get in tune with myself. And the Anthony Gilardi Acting Studio, particularly Anthony Gilardi, for always giving me a safe home to express myself.

My family and my friends, who have always been there for me. I'm so lucky to have friends who are like family and if I was to name each and every one, I would still be here writing this in a month's time! Thank you for always supporting me in whatever I do. Also, a big thank you to my dog Duke. I love you more than I love cookie dough.

My publishers for giving me the opportunity to tell my story. In particular, thanks to my editors Deepthi Talwar and Kushalrani Gulab for making my writing coherent.

Thanks also Aunty Tush for just being you and Noah Baron for helping put my original notes together.

And finally thank you to everyone who reached out and supported me through the whole ConSIDer This series. You inspired me to write this book!